A LIFE MORE THAN
Ordinary

ONE WOMAN'S TRUE STORY
ABOUT LOVE, LOSS, & *HOPE*
IN A FAITHFUL GOD

JULIE TYRIE

Ark House Press
arkhousepress.com

© 2025 Julie Tyrie | First edition 2013

Cataloguing in Publication Data:
Title: A Life More Than Ordinary
ISBN: 9780987388896 (pbk.)
Subjects: Spiritual, Biography
Other Authors/Contributors: Tyrie, Julie

Design and layout by initiateagency.com

Not to us, LORD, not to us but to your name be the glory, because of your love and faithfulness.

–Psalm 115:1, (NIV)

This book is dedicated to my late husband, Neil Garry Tyrie.
This book is part of his legacy. Our life together, his death,
and his reward set the context: Eternity matters.

Contents

Acknowledgements

There are so many people to thank—there is no way that I can give this task the justice it deserves. Can I just say that if you know me and I know your name, I thank you for the input that you have had in my life, for being a support, a mirror, a reminder, a counsellor, a friend. I have often said that the truest evidence of God's blessing in my life is seen in the people whom He has placed in my life. I dearly love all of my friends, family, and acquaintances, and am aware that my life is richer for having them in it. However, I would particularly like to thank the following people for the positive influence and blessing that they have been in my life:

To Jimbo and Alice Mitchison, Rob and Jenny Mitchison, and Maurie (deceased) and Liz Beard: Thank you so much for putting God's love into action and rescuing me. Your love, patience, generosity and constant prayers have set me on the path that I walk on today. My life is your legacy.

To my family, Mum; Monika and Trev, and their beautiful girls, Aliesha and Jayde; Scott; and little Trevor: I love you all and am so glad that I can share my life with you. Thank you for all of your support and love.

To the Tyrie family, Garry and Shirley Tyrie; Wayne and Kathy Tyrie, and their children, Maddison, Hayden, Mitchell, and Kyllum; and Loren Tyrie: Thank you for every action and every word that has been done out of the love that you have for Neil and his girls.

To my dearest friends who have always been there, always loved me, always supported me through even the toughest times, Joanne and Max Barnes, Robyn and John Pattison, Ronda and Paddy

Gladwell, Sharon and John Dein, Sue and Craig Day, Eileen Smith, Vicki Taylor, Sally Smith, and Bronwyn Mergard: You have all made my life richer and have encouraged me greatly at the perfect time. Thank you for your love and support in my darkest hours; you have never failed me.

To Amanda and Mark Burnett: You have always been my biggest fan club. Thank you!

To my spiritual mentor, Sharon Wilks: Your encouragement and belief in me encourages me to see God's bigger picture and has reinforced to me that God does have 'greater things' for me to do.

To my church family: Thank you for every prayer, every meal, every working bee in my yard, every kind word and thought, and for loving my girls and me through our winter as well as through our spring and summer—in other words, thank you for outworking God's love toward us. I love you all dearly.

To Victoria Purdie (www.purdiephotography.com): Thank you for all of your help and support with photography and with editing the photographs contained within this book. You have been such a blessing to me.

To the staff at Christian Heritage College, Mansfield: You still are, and always will be, my favourite bunch of academics! Your recognition of my potential will never be forgotten, and your support during my darkest times speaks volumes of the love of God that dwells in you. My journey with you all altered my course for the better and allowed me to be the person that God destined me to be.

To Matt and Nicole Danswan, and staff at Ark House Press: Thank you for taking on my book and believing in me, an unknown author, and giving me the opportunity to preach God's Word. I know that our partnership aligns with God's will to see His name praised!

To my beautiful girls, Emmy, Maya and Callie: This book is for you, to show you what happens when we put our trust, hope, and faith in a God who never ever lets us down. This is a record of your lives so far, that you may be reminded in years to come of the father you lost and will see again, of the mother who wishes—more than anything—to be a godly model who you can follow, and of the heritage that is yours as children of God. Maya, never forget what a special miracle you are. Let that colour everything that you see in the life that you have been blessed with. I love you girls so much, and I am so proud of you all. Thank you for your love, support, encouragement, and hugs as we have all celebrated through the process of writing this book.

And finally, to the one who deserves all praise, honour, and glory, to my loving Heavenly Father: You truly are a 'father to the fatherless'. Thank you for never letting me down—ever. My life is Yours and always will be. My heart will always declare the love that I have for You; and my thoughts, intents, and actions will seek to align with that declaration through Your intervention and Your power in my life.

Introduction

This is a book that I had to write, not because the umpteenth person told me to write it, although that did happen, but rather, I had to write this book because I truly felt that it was God's will for me to do so. To not write the book would signal my turning from Ninevah and indicate my running towards Tarshish. If I have learnt anything in this life, it is that being in God's will is not only the safest, most rewarding place to be, but it is where we recognise our destinies. Therefore, with a heart open to God's leading by His Holy Spirit, I have endeavoured to put into the book only the words that I felt were meant to be contained within it. Even though the book contains difficult journeys through which I have travelled, the purpose of this book is not to place blame, air bitterness, or highlight my own strength or ability. Instead, the purpose of this book is to bring glory to the Almighty God, who is deserving of all of our lives *and more*. This means that there are experiences in my life that are omitted from this book. This is not done to present a story that is false or incomplete, but rather, it is done so that the book stays true to its purpose and becomes a blessing and a win-win for all. It is my hope that, in the pages of this book, you will either be introduced to, reacquainted with, and/or reminded of, the faithfulness of God to keep, protect, and care for us through life.

The title of this book, *A Life More than Ordinary* actually began as *A Life Less Than Ordinary*, summing up in one sentence that my life has been unique because of my struggles. However, in creating the title, I felt strongly that I should change the word 'less' to 'more' because even though I have not had an easy life, it has been truly blessed. So, yes, my life has been 'more than ordinary'. However,

I do not in any way wish to communicate that I am unique in my struggles. Unfortunately, there are many who could challenge me on how difficult their lives have been. As a history teacher, I am well aware of the struggles, hardships, and atrocities faced by many and the difficult and often ultimate sacrifices made by those wanting to make the world better for others. Despite this, I felt that I had something valuable to share, and I have, and always will, jump at any opportunity to communicate how amazing, loving, faithful, beautiful, and magnificent my God is.

I have known throughout the process of writing this book that someday someone will read this and hear what he or she was destined by God to hear, someone that I will probably never meet. It has been my strongest desire to highlight the message of hope that is available to all who know God in a personal, relational way. The thesis of this book is that no matter what you go through in life, when you keep a steady focus on God, you can not only get through it but do so whilst feeling the love, peace, joy, and assurance that our loving God gives.

In writing this book, I have questioned how anyone, including myself, can truly convey the magnificence of the Almighty God, the Creator of the universe. I must say, I feel unworthy to accept such a challenge, but I have written from my heart and spirit what I know to be true and what I know to be Truth. I hope that that is enough. Dear reader, no matter what, no matter when, no matter how life shows up for you, God's love never fails. Period.

Content warning
The purpose of this autobiography is to inspire and encourage. However, in sharing my life story, I do refer to the topics of domestic violence, childhood abuse and neglect, bullying, terminal illness, death, and grief. While I have tried to avoid giving graphic details, please be kind to yourself and seek help if necessary. Love and blessings!

Chapter One

MY JOURNEY BEGINS

Day by day the Lord takes care of the innocent, and they will receive an inheritance that lasts forever. They will not be disgraced in hard times; even in famine they will have more than enough

Psalm 37:18-19 (New Living Translation)

··•

Regardless of where one sits in the nature versus nurture debate, it is obvious that one's life experiences have an indelible effect on one's perspective and attitudes in life. One who has an easy life may walk through life believing that the world is their oyster, a veritable mecca of opportunities waiting to be realised. However, in the other extreme, one who has grown up with survival as the main goal may see life as a battle to endure, a race to finish rather than a race to win. As a result of my life experiences, I have, for most of my life, seen my survival, and the survival of those close to me, as the ultimate goal. My perspective on life was tainted; from early on I had to learn to survive on my own, to look to myself as the only thing that I could count on in a world that was in chaos.

I have often wondered what sort of person I would have become if my life experiences had been different, more agreeable. Would I have realised my talents and abilities earlier if someone had noticed that I possessed them? In looking back on my earliest memories, albeit few, I sensed my isolation. Even at a young age, I knew that my circumstances were less than ideal. However, before I go into detail on my upbringing, I wish to make clear that despite my trials, I dearly love my mother, and my father, who has since passed away. Each one of us tries to do the best with what we have gained and understood in this life. Vices and weaknesses can plague us all; who are any of us to judge? My parents did the best that they could with what they had, and I do not just mean in a physical sense. Perhaps in making this statement, I focus more on the metaphysical, the things that are apart from what we can see.

My father, Trevor, the son of an alcoholic father, himself became enslaved to the addiction. From an early age, he was violent and aggressive. Before he met my mum, Janet (Jan), he had a family—a wife and two sons—who, whilst Dad was passed out on the floor drunk, fled and never returned. His wife knew too well his brutality, having been hospitalised more than once as a result of his violent nature. Soon after, my father met my mum, a teenage runaway, and before they married in 1974, I was conceived. I was born in January 1975 and named Julie Ann Hardy. My sister, Monika, arrived a year later, followed by my brother, Scott, again a year later; then, two years later, the fourth child, my younger brother, Trevor Jr, was born.

To be honest, I do not remember a lot of my early childhood; it is a series of stilted pictures and snapshots of negative information framed within fear. I remember enough to know that we lived in squalor, in a situation that was barely liveable. Even though we lived in a unit block in the late 70s in Tuncurry, New South Wales, I remember that we did not have a flushing toilet, but, instead, used a bucket to go to the toilet in. I vaguely remember being surrounded by less-than-savoury persons who frequented my family home, mostly to drink with, and take advantage of, my far too generous father.

In looking back, I still sense the fear and the dread that was my constant companion, and I am sure that there is a reason why I remember so little. I do recall vividly my father arguing with my mum. I remember him throwing a kitchen table at her, and I remember running down the street with my mum, my sister, and my two brothers, escaping to Nan and Pop's home over on the next street; this was not uncommon. I can remember to this day the driveways of the houses that we ran over, and how, with my little legs, I had to leap over the wheel tracks to meet the next patch of grass. In later years, I was astonished by how small the distance was between the wheel tracks that at the time had seemed huge and a great effort to reach. Unfortunately, episodes like this were a part of daily and weekly life. I remember one of my aunties, my dad's older sister, jumping on the bonnet of our car, one of the very few that we ever owned, and yelling at my dad to not drive off because he was drunk and had a disqualified licence as a result of drunken driving.

I recall going to Tuncurry Primary School, both the new and the old, and I felt isolated, had few if any friends, and remember being bullied. It seems that I did my very best to disappear and to remain unnoticed in whichever situation I found myself; that was the safest option.

My only source of comfort for those first five or six years of my life was my paternal grandmother, my nan, Orita, who I adored, who won beauty contests in her youth, always wore make-up, and had Grace Kelly elegance. She was a stunningly beautiful women who, due to a difficult life, wore hard-won resilience with humility and grace. She worried incessantly for her young grandchildren and did the best she could to keep us safe whilst loving her troubled son. I have been told numerous times by extended family members that I take after my nan. A higher compliment cannot be paid. My nan was a Worimi woman, a close descendant of a well-known Indigenous elder on the Wallis Lake with the surname Cunningham whose life is recorded in articles in the local Tuncurry Museum. Nan's mother, Ruth Cunningham, married a white man named Percy Croker. Despite me being constantly surrounded by Indigenous people throughout my childhood, and having Indigenous school friends tell me I was Indigenous, sadly, my Indigenous heritage wasn't confirmed to me til I was thirty-one years old and at my nan's funeral in 2006. I approached a group of dark-skinned Indigenous women and asked them how they knew my nan and they explained that they were her first cousins. The confusion about my heritage was partly due to two of my dad's sisters fighting throughout my childhood about whether we were Indigenous or not and I never knew who to believe. The other reason was that I had fair skin, freckles, and red hair, having taken after my red-headed mother whose grandmother and grandfather were born in England and Scotland respectively. Dad's father, Jack, my pop, was a white man who was born in Greymouth, New Zealand. His family moved to Australia when he was a baby and settled in Failford near Tuncurry. Sadly, I have found it hard to embrace my heritage as being part Indigenous due to experiencing and witnessing a lot of abuse and systemic issues arising from the Indigenous culture. In fact, even as an adult, I experience fear-based physical reactions when seeing Indigenous people, particularly men. However, I personally know some beautiful Christian Indigenous people who had a profoundly positive impact on my early life and, over the years, I have made steps towards reconciling with my Indigenous heritage with the hope of celebrating and embracing it proudly.

In 1981, when I was age six, we moved from Tuncurry to Taree, away from my nan and all she represented. We moved into a brand-new housing commission house, which was like a mansion to me. I can still vividly remember driving into the driveway in our beat-up old car, looking out the window and staring up at my new home. The move meant a new school, Taree Primary School. However, the location was all that was new; the bullying continued, and not just for me, but also for my sister and brothers. We were easy targets, quiet, dishevelled, dirty, out of uniform, and without parental presence.

I was glad to leave that school when a new school, Manning Gardens Public School, opened up down the road from our house in 1984. I have many more memories about this time in my life; however, it was more of the same. Whilst at this school, I was bullied and occasionally pulled out of class to have my head lice dealt with. My parents were questioned about the food in my lunch box—that was when I actually did bring food to school—and I remember many instances in which other students' parents came to special events at the school and my parents never turned up. It got to a stage where I never expected them to. At this time, I also remember my father fronting up to court for varying charges, the Child Safety Department checking up on us, and students at school teasing me by saying that they found out that I was adopted and me wishing more than anything that what they said was true.

On the home front, things were very volatile; we all lived like we were walking on eggshells, my mum, my siblings, and me. World War III descended on our home approximately every week or so for ten years, always starting with the smell of alcohol. I remember my mum having black eyes, and I remember my mum trying to stop my dad from hitting my brothers, which happened constantly; they reminded him too much of himself. My sister, who was an attractive blue-eyed blonde, was the recipient of my dad's verbal abuse; as a pretty girl she was bound to get herself into trouble, although she never did. I was the lucky one, if you could call it that. I was Dad's favourite; I did well at school, stayed out of trouble, and knew how to keep the peace. However, my experience of that time involved the occasional tirade of verbal abuse from my father, the neglect of my mum who struggled with the situation, and the witness of too many things that a young child should never have to hear or see, which will remain with me and me alone. Because my mother had her own problems dealing with an abusive husband, I was on my own, doing my best, as the oldest sibling, to look after my sister and brothers.

My father, despite his vices, was a very hard worker. He worked as an oyster farmer, like his father before him, leaving the house early six days a week to be driven by his brother, also an oyster farmer, to Forster–Tuncurry to work on Wallis Lake. My favourite memories of my dad were either before he went to work in the morning, or just after he arrived home from work, because they were the only times that he was sober. Other than those few redeeming times, my father was on the verge of being abusive, or actually being abusive, or trying to fix the consequences of his abuse with his many excuses. In his early days, my dad was a boxer and, in his older age and in his delirium, he still fancied himself as one. I recall countless times that he would come home from the local pubs covered in blood from taking on an opponent who was too big. He would generally end up lying on the lounge room floor feeling sorry for himself before he finally passed out.

Probably the most vivid memory that I have of my childhood was one argument between Mum and Dad that became particularly violent. My sister, brothers, and I ran to find safe havens in and around the house. I hid under a large, overgrown elephant ear plant in the garden next to the house, listening to my dad yelling at my mum, and hearing things break in the house. I was worried about my sister and brothers because in the scramble I lost sight of them. Next thing, I heard the next-door neighbour calling to me to come over to the fence. I ran over and he lifted me over the fence, where I saw my sister and brothers. We waited it out there in the neighbour's home until things died down, which they always eventually did—til next time.

Somewhere amongst all of this, I was rescued. It was around 1983, and an elderly couple was visiting my part of town—the worst part. They came to the door and introduced themselves as Mr and Mrs Beardsly, pastors of the local Assemblies of God church. They were wondering if my parents would allow my sister, brothers, and me to go to Sunday school. I am not sure if it was because my dad was raised by a believing mother or because my parents were keen to get rid of us, but we began to go to Sunday school, and my romance with my Almighty God began.

Chapter Two

RESCUE

My help comes from the LORD, who made the heaven and the earth! He will not let you stumble; the one who watches over you will not slumber

Psalm 121:2-3 (NLT)

....•

To me, it was not just going to Sunday school; I felt that I had found the missing piece of the puzzle. I found something that was stable. I rested in the constancy of God's love for me, a love that was unconditional. Even at a young age, I felt God's presence all around me, and as a result, I was able to endure with hope, from that moment on, the trials that I faced in my home environment. I was no longer alone, and I knew that I had a future and a hope (Jeremiah 29:11).

One of the greatest examples of God's faithfulness to me came in the form of a family in the church—the Mitchison family. Jim (Jimbo) and Alice Mitchison, a married couple in their sixties at the time, took me under their wing and set me on the spiritual path that I now walk on. They owned vast and picture-perfect farming land in Tinonee, near Taree, where they grew beans and snow peas and farmed beef cattle. Their married children, Rob and Jenny Mitchison, and Maurie and Liz Beard, also lived and worked on the property. They also took on the role of caring for me. My regular attendance at church in the first ten years of my romance with God was a result of Alice diligently picking my sister, brothers and I up in her car and taking us to church. The Mitchisons' care for me continued with trips out to their farm after church on Sundays, which then became weekend stay overs, and then finally, when I was in my mid-teens, I lived with Alice and Jimbo and worked on their farm for around six months. I owe so much of who I am to this wonderful family, who I am still in contact with.

To be out of the hostile environment that I grew up in and to be amongst people who loved God as I did was such a relief and a life-changing blessing. In fact, I saw myself as being a lot like Anne from *Anne of Green Gables*. Actually, when I was introduced to Anne in my late teens, I realised I *was* Anne Shirley. I was a dirty, skinny, neglected young girl with fair skin, freckles and red hair who was also rescued by an elderly couple to live and work on their farm. Like Anne, I loved literature and was a hopeless romantic. I could easily see myself quoting Tennyson's 'The Lady of Shalott' while lying in a sinking boat on the river, and I shared her hatred of red hair. It was definitely not cool to have red hair in the 80s and 90s. And while I do have the middle name 'Ann', I have always been disappointed that it does not end with an 'e'.

During my stay with Alice and Jimbo, I learnt how to cook, clean, manage my finances, as well as how to be hygienic—the lessons that I never learnt at home. As a youngster, I remember watching with awe as Alice mopped the floor. I watched her put the mop in and out of the bucket of water and then onto the dirty floor. In my naivety, I asked her why she was putting dirty water onto her floor. I also learnt the names of different vegetables, how to tell the difference between a cucumber and a zucchini, as well as what utensils to use in the kitchen. Even though all of these things were a necessity, and I have always been grateful for this instruction given through simple modelling, what I treasure the most are the memories of the Bible readings that we sat down to after every evening meal, and the prayers that were prayed. It was in these times that my faith became practical and long-lasting. The Mitchisons' love for me, a snotty-nosed, dirty little kid, and their willingness to sacrifice their time for me so that God's will would come to fruition in my life, will always be remembered with the wholehearted gratefulness it deserves. When visiting Jimbo and Alice many years later, Jimbo told me that not a day had passed when he had not prayed for me. God used the Mitchison family to set me on the right path, and it has spoken volumes to me over the years of His faithfulness to save and deliver me.

Due to God's overwhelming love and provision, as well as the influence of the Mitchison family, I became an avid scholar of God's Word, and I set myself apart. In doing so, I enlarged the difference between my peers and myself, as well as between my family and myself. There I was, a committed Christian living daily in an environment of drugs, alcohol, pornography, and violence. I continued in the church throughout my teenage years, eventually changing churches and becoming a member of the Christian Outreach Centre in Taree in 1991.

Even though I thrived in the church and in my relationship with God, I had my problems. I had no self-esteem, I did not see my worth, I struggled with my identity, and I lived in constant fear. In fact, fear ruled my life for many years. I withdrew within myself, and I was constantly in survival mode, trying to protect myself. My fear was so constricting that as a small child, I remember I was too scared to leave my room, and as a result went to the toilet on the floor in my bedroom. It has only been in recent years that I have dealt with the fear that constricted me so much that I barely functioned, and when I did, I was on autopilot. In other words, I existed because I drew breath, but that was all. My heart had long decided that there was little joy and security in life, and the goal of every day was to survive and be invisible.

In 1990, after my father had been kicked out of the family home by my mum on numerous occasions, and then subsequently welcomed back, my dad left the house for the last time; Mum had finally had enough and refused to take him back. I was fifteen years old. From that moment on, my life at home became far easier; however, Mum still was in and out of relationship with my dad, but they lived in separate locations. She usually left us at home when staying with my father on weekends.

I was a very dedicated Christian in my teenage years, choosing not to date, choosing to immerse myself in God one hundred percent. He was still the constant that I needed. He was my protector, my refuge, my safe harbour. There were many situations where God rescued me from danger and harm throughout my childhood and teenage years. For example, we lived in the worst part of town with unsavoury people. One night, in my early teens, while I slept in the bedroom that I shared with my sister, a man attempted to break into the room through a broken window that would not lock, no screen, no obstacles. My sister tried to wake me, but I continued to sleep. In the morning, my sister explained what had happened, saying that after the man started to climb in the window, he stopped suddenly, and then he jumped down from the window. She heard him run into the old cubby house in the corner of the backyard as he ran to the back fence and jumped over it, fleeing. To this day I do not know what he saw or heard, but I am sure it was not earthly! I experienced many situations like this, some even more dangerous. It was a continual confirmation to me of the will of God to protect and keep me, regardless of my circumstances. This evidence of God's love and provision went on, in my future life, to become the thing that I hung my existence on. When God moves heaven and earth to protect you in an environment that is volatile and dangerous, you know without a doubt that you can endure all things when He is by your side.

Today, I am still in relationship with my family. However, my father passed away on 14 November 2009, after a long battle with cancer. I continued a long-distance relationship with my dad up until his death; he was a man with vices and weaknesses, but he was also a man with a big heart. I chose not to exhibit animosity toward my father for his actions and shortcomings. To me, he was a man gripped by an addiction that he could not escape from, despite going into rehabilitation facilities on more than one occasion later in his life. As a Christian, I forgave him and loved him, choosing to see him the way that God saw him. I am grateful that I was with him even as he lay on his deathbed. Today, I have a great relationship with my sister and her family, as well as my two brothers, all who I see at Christmastime, as they live far from me. My mum has become a vital part of my family unit. I am very proud of the person that she has become, having stepped out from underneath the bondage of abuse.

Each of us has a story or two to share about our struggles with past events. To this day, my youngest brother will not look anyone in the eye. We have all struggled with realising our worth and value. It is not my place to share any struggles and vices my siblings may have experienced as a result of our upbringing; it is my hope and prayer that someday they will be freed from any chains and bondages that may inhibit them.

Chapter Three

A NEW LIFE

He lifted me out of the pit of despair,
out of the mud and the mire.
He set my feet on solid ground and
steadied me as I walked along

Psalm 40:2 (NLT)

....•

As a young lady of seventeen, I began working at the local
hardware store, Taree Mitre 10. It was due to this that I
ceased to live with the Mitchison family and moved back
in with my mum. By the time I was nineteen, I was managing a
department in the store. In fact, I managed the kitchenware
department, and it was there that I put all of my newly-acquired
knowledge about running a home and working in a kitchen to good
use. It never ceases to amaze me how faithful God is to look after
even the little things. With God, nothing is a coincidence.

At that time, I had refused any advances by young gentlemen who
were not 'marriage material' and then a thin six-feet-four-inches-tall
gentleman from my church came along, showing an interest in me.
His name was Neil Garry Tyrie, and after a short courtship, we were
engaged, and after a six-month engagement, we were married on
20 May 1995. I was twenty years old, and he was twenty-eight. It
was Neil's sense of humour that drew me to him. I knew of him

because he was a brother to my friend Loren. At that time, he lived in Sydney, helping out a church there. I remember when he first came back to live at his family's property at Upper Lansdowne. He had made a statement in our youth group gathering that God had told him to come back because he was to get married. At the time, I was amazed and perplexed by his confidence. Over the months, after Neil's return, neither of us had an interest in each other. In fact, we disliked each other. I saw him down the street once, and he asked if I would help him put up posters advertising a Christian concert that was coming up. I said I would. Listening to him talk as we drove around, I thought to myself, 'This is the rudest man I have ever met!', and I was happy to walk away from him at the end of the chore. Later, when we started dating, he told me that he had been deliberately rude because he had not wanted me to like him. There was no chance of that! But God had other plans.

One time, when some members of the youth group from church were giving Neil, who was twenty-seven at the time, a hard time about being 'old' and single, calling him 'Methuselah', I prayed with heartfelt conviction that God would bless him with a good wife. I said 'Amen' and forgot about it. Then, one night after church, as I was hanging out in the coffee area, I felt God tell me to make Neil a cup of tea. So, I went and asked him how he liked his tea, made it for him, gave it to him, and again forgot about it, going back to my previous conversation with my friend. Neil later went on a mission trip to Vanuatu. He later told me that whilst there, he felt like God hit him on the head, and he thought, 'Julie is not too bad a girl. I'm going to chase her up when I get back.' And he did.

My most memorable moment of our courtship occurred one evening in the coffee area of our church after the service. There I was, sitting between two men, one being Neil. At the time, Neil had a beard, which he had kept from the mission trip, as did the man on the other side of me. Neil, being Neil, cheekily said, 'Look, three people in a row with moustaches!' His humour and outright disregard for propriety won me over. However, despite his roughish side, I thought him to be very spiritual and mature. The more I got to know him, the less I thought that. Once we were married, I used to joke that I was mature for my age and Neil was immature for his, so we met nicely in the middle. Despite Neil's roughish disregard for propriety, there was no escaping that God seemed to be in our union. In 1990, whilst at Bible College, Neil prayed and fasted for his future bride. Later we realised that that was when my dad had left home for the last time, which made my life a lot easier. Further, before we met, Neil felt strongly to make a vow to God to not drink alcohol. God knew that I could not be in a relationship with a man who drank, the smell alone would have sent me into a state of panic.

We got married 20 May 1995, and it was nice to escape the family home that I had known all my life and finally be in control of my surroundings. In our first year of marriage, we were surrounded by family and spent a lot of time on Neil's family's three-generation-owned former dairy farm in Upper Lansdowne, near Taree. The views from the family home boasted lush, green paddocks of grazing beef cattle, bordered by a creek and magnificent blue-tinged mountains.

After a year, in May 1996, we moved out west to the small cotton-farming community of Wee Waa, New South Wales, population of 1,860, where Neil had originally grown up and worked as a teenager. Being a coastal girl, it was definitely a change of pace and culture for me, and the vast, red soil plains and paddocks were nothing like the rolling, green hills I was used to on the Mitchison farm that resembled those surrounding Anne Shirley's Green Gables. During the three years that we were there, Neil worked on cotton farms, furrowing paddocks and growing cotton. He also became a cotton-picking contractor. And I, having received a transfer from my job in Taree, worked at the Mitre 10 hardware store in Narrabri, fifty kilometres away, and I worked for a while as an administration and payroll clerk in the local supermarket in Wee Waa.

We were established in the local Christian Outreach Centre church in Narrabri and were surrounded and supported by an amazing community of people with country ways. As a result of the country hospitality freely offered to me, I began to flourish and open up, allowing people to see the real me. I built friendships with people and started to see my own worth. I loved living out west, with its simple life. I took long walks on the cotton farm we lived on, and I never quite got used to seeing some of Australia's most venomous snakes, as well as emus, kangaroos, and wild boars while I roamed. In fact, it was nothing to be cooking in the kitchen and see a huge, wild pig trotting through the yard. Country living suited me well, and I became a proficient country cook. Out west, nobody buys premade biscuits and cakes for meetings and catch-up sessions; everything is homemade. The nearest take-away store was almost a thirty-minute drive away, so every meal was of the hearty, home-cooked variety.

During this time, I fell pregnant with our first child, a daughter, Emmy Rose, born on 2 March 1998. She had her mother's red hair and big almond eyes, but instead of having her mother's hazel eyes, she had her father's striking blue eyes. We enjoyed our little family in our little home on the farm until we were asked to become senior pastors of the Christian Outreach Centre church in Wellington, New South Wales. We left Wee Waa and our church family and friends and moved to Wellington in April 1999, with little Emmy in tow. She had recently turned one and was walking around on wobbly legs. With us came our beloved dog, Marla, whom we had acquired in our time in Wee Waa; she was a beautiful, loyal Rhodesian Ridgeback.

Both Neil and I, living out of a committed relationship with our beloved God, were keen to make the most of the opportunity that we had to serve in the church at Wellington. We did so to the best of our abilities and then relied on God for the rest. An amazing group of people in the church supported us, and Neil flourished in his role, caring for his flock and delivering powerful messages in his preaching, being led by the Holy Spirit. It was not all roses, as anyone in full-time ministry will attest to. There are many pressures and struggles both on earth and in the spirit realm when you are on the front line, and in many ways, we were newbies. Further, the pressure on our family unit and our marriage was palpable, even destructive at times, but we got through it, working hard to protect and maintain our relationship.

Not long after we arrived in Wellington, we discovered that we were expecting our second child. Another daughter, Maya Grace, was born on 18 February 2000, a millennium baby who came out of the womb with strikingly beautiful features. She, like her older sister, had her father's bright blue eyes, but they were framed with dark eyebrows and eyelashes that created the perfect contrast against her lily-white skin. Only the first-born female of every generation had red hair—that being my mum's mum, my mum, me, and Emmy—so Maya had her father's brown hair. She was a welcome addition to our little family unit as we served as a family in the church. Little did we know at the time what the arrival of our second daughter would herald in the near future. The name Maya in Hindi means 'illusion' or 'dream'. She certainly lived up to her name, taking us on a journey that seemed at best, surreal, and at worst, a nightmare.

Chapter Four

GOING INTO BATTLE

The LORD is close to the brokenhearted and saves those who are crushed in spirit

Psalm 34:18 (NIV)

W hen Maya was born, the doctors and nurses noticed that she had a little lump in the right side of her buttocks, discovered when they did the initial check upon birth. At four days old, she had an ultrasound. The overseeing doctor, who had delivered her, decided that the lump was a cystic hygroma, a large lymphangioma that is a benign sac of lymphatic fluid. Maya was put into the medical system, where she was monitored by a specialist doctor who travelled from Sydney to the regional areas. As Maya developed and grew into a happy, squealing little bub, we drove an hour and a half to the regional city of Orange, New South Wales, to see the doctor once every three months. Over time, the lump in her backside grew larger, apparently filling with more fluid. We held discussions with the doctor about possible treatments. I vividly recall asking the doctor at one of our appointments if it could be cancer. His definitive 'No' came as a big relief to me. He was a specialist from the big city; he would know what he was talking about. The months wore on, and when Maya was around ten months old, we started to get very concerned. The lump was growing at a rapid rate, and she wasn't doing all the things that her sister, Emmy, had done at that age. However, the biggest trigger for concern was that our bubbly, carefree little girl was unsettled, frustrated, and seemed to be in pain. As the lump grew, she became more uncomfortable sitting up; we had to prop her up on a towel in the car seat and in the high chair. All this time, she was being monitored by the doctor from Sydney who always sent us away with a smile, saying, 'See you in three months.' Out of desperation, we took Maya back to the local doctor who had delivered her. He was astounded by the size of the lump, which had now grown to the size of a rockmelon off her backside and had appeared in her groin as a lump the size of a golf ball. The doctor contacted The Children's Hospital at Westmead in Sydney to request an emergency MRI, which she was scheduled to have at a later date. At this time, it was difficult to get hold of a specialist, as they were all on Christmas break, including the specialist doctor we were seeing regularly. The general practitioner called in a favour from a friend who was a plastic surgeon who worked at the The Children's Hospital at Westmead. He agreed to come in on his holiday and look over the results of the MRI. So, we packed up for a two-day trip to the city, Neil, Emmy, Maya and I. The doctors performed the MRI and we met with the plastic surgeon to discuss the results. He could not find an office that was available to use, so we went into the RN's office on a nearby ward. The doctor was yet to see the results and waited along with us as the images finally flicked up on the computer screen. He was quiet for a time as he viewed the results. Then, he turned to look at us and stated, 'Well, it is not going to be as easy to deal with as I thought.' He then went on to tell us to go home for the weekend, which happened to include my twenty-sixth birthday, and then come back down to the hospital to have the lump removed from her groin. Off we went home, with few cares, to enjoy the weekend, serve in the church, and pack to go back to the hospital on Monday. As I left on that memorable Monday morning to go back to the hospital, little did I realise that it would be the last time that I would walk out the door of that house.

When we arrived at The Children's Hospital at Westmead, Maya was admitted onto the surgical ward, aptly named 'Faithful Ward'. She was scheduled to go into surgery the next day. Neil's mum, Shirley, drove down from the family farm to be there and support us. On the day of the surgery, which I can remember as clearly as if it happened yesterday, we were sitting in a small interview room, to which we had been directed after being told that Maya was out of surgery and in the recovery room, and we were waiting. The room was empty except for two chairs, a table, and a box of tissues. I recall noticing the box of tissues and making a light remark to Neil, something to the effect that this must be the room where they bring parents to tell them that things did not go so well in surgery for their children. Neil nodded. Within minutes of my statement, in walked three men dressed in dark suits and ties, holding briefcases; one of them was the specialist we had been seeing every three months or so. Whilst standing, the specialist looked at us and said, 'Well . . . it's cancer'. After that statement I am sure he said other things pertaining to what would happen next; however, I never really got past those first three words. We later found out that Maya was diagnosed as having a stage four germ cell tumour, which generally occur during the development of the embryo, resulting in a birth defect. Hers had arisen from a sacrococcygeal teratoma, a tumour located near the tailbone, the most common tumour presenting in newborns.

Neil and I held it together and watched as the doctor left the room with his entourage. Except for seeing him months later in the hospital elevator where he did not acknowledge or recognise me, I never saw him again.

At this point in retelling my life story, I feel incapable of putting into words how I felt in that moment of being told that my beautiful daughter, eleven months old, had cancer; not only that, but that she had obviously battled with it for quite some time under our watchful, careful gaze. A nurse came into the little room and told us that we could go into the recovery area to see Maya, who had woken up. When I sat beside the hospital bed, picked up my innocent little girl, and tried to understand what this news meant for her, I lost all composure and wept whilst Neil sat beside me and Maya looked up at me with her beautiful blue eyes framed in dark lashes. I knew in that moment that our lives had been directed onto a different path, an unexpected, unknown journey that would require from us everything that we had and more. We followed Maya back onto the ward as the orderly pushed her in her hospital bed. We saw Neil's mum on our travels and broke the news to her through tears.

When we got to the hospital room, there were already brochures and cards from the hospital chaplains lying on the bed. You see, when the doctor had sat down with us and looked at the screen on the previous Friday, he had known then the battle we were about to face; it was no surprise to anyone, not the nurses nor all the specialist doctors. It was no surprise to anyone but us. Neil's brother, Wayne, flew down from Brisbane to support us, and both he and Neil's father, Garry, who had also arrived, went back to Wellington to collect some clothes and other supplies for our unforeseen, extended stay. They brought back with them a framed photo of Emmy, Maya and me, taken on Christmas Day, four weeks before. Marla, our beloved dog, went to stay with our dear friends, the Pattisons, on their farm near Narrabri, which became her permanent home.

Chapter Five

THE BATTLE RAGES

*Though an army besiege me, my heart will not
fear; though war break out against me,
even then I will be confident*

Psalm 27:3 (NIV)

....●

On learning of Maya's diagnosis, we were introduced to Maya's oncologist, Dr Luciano Dalla-Pozza, a kind, humorous, and caring Italian man we lovingly called Luc. He made a few phone calls and got our family into Ronald McDonald House, a home away from home for families with sick children, sponsored by the McDonald's restaurant franchise. It was situated within the hospital grounds, and it became a safe haven for our family, as well as numerous other families who were battling to keep their children with them. Over our time there, we met some amazing people, the staff included, but most amazing were the sick and terminally-ill children who we met and came to love.

Luc came to Maya's hospital room two days after her diagnosis. We were sitting with her in the room, surrounded by family members. He asked Neil and me to come aside with him, so we followed him out of the room. He sat us down in an empty room and explained that the cancer was a mass that extended from the pubic bone in the front to protrude out of her backside, from one hip bone across to the other hip bone, and had also spread to her ankle, her spine, and her lung. He then went on to tell us that medical testing showed that as a result of the cancer in her spine, her right leg was totally paralysed, as was her bladder; her wet nappies were a result of an overfull bladder. He then explained that she had a ten percent chance of surviving. However, it would not be the cancer that would kill her in the event of her death, it would be the treatment.

Chemotherapy kills the cancer at the same time as it attacks the organs and other parts of the body, particularly the fastest-growing cells. This is why patients often lose their hair and suffer from mouth ulcers. After receiving the results of testing, the chemotherapy protocol the doctors decided upon took into account which parts of Maya's body were healthy enough to hopefully withstand the attack she was about to face. A protocol is the regime of drugs that are used, the sequence they are used in, and how much. This is balanced with the amount of maintenance fluids that will be pumped in to flush out the harmful chemicals when they have done their job.

Her heart was already showing signs of stress, so they decided that her kidneys would bear the brunt of the attack instead; they looked healthy. All of this news, her paralysis and her supposed prognosis, swept over me like a similar wave to what I had experienced only days before. Could it get much worse? Neil and I thanked Luc, and we walked into the hospital room to give the news to the family.

Except for Neil's family, who had come to the hospital, I could not tell my best friends or my family the news of Maya's diagnosis for the first week or so. It was impossible for me in those early days to even voice the predicament in which we suddenly found ourselves. Eventually, I rang my dear friends in Narrabri, Max and Joanne Barnes, and John and Robyn Pattison, and they became a huge support to Neil and me throughout our battle, calling us every week to encourage us and to get an update to pass on to the praying church at Narrabri. Because we were senior pastors of a church, many churches across the denomination rose up in prayer on our behalf, and we felt the support and the covering.

In the beginning, when Luc spoke of the chemotherapy that

Maya would be having, I had no idea what that even entailed. I had visions of her being put in a room and then gassed, or something to that effect. The first time our little baby girl had chemotherapy was certainly an eye-opener, and if I had been living in denial up to that point, the situation was certainly clarified for me. Chemotherapy comes in different forms: liquid, tablet, and in this case, Maya had intravenous (liquid) chemotherapy delivered into a central line. Maya had an operation in the first week to put in this central line, which looked like an upside-down letter 'y'. It was made up of exterior tubes that connected internally to her blood system so that drugs and fluids could be intravenously put in, two or more at a time, and blood could be taken out for testing without using needles. Neil and I had to clean the central line twice a day, using a very specific procedure, to help avoid infection. As part of this maintenance, the nurses would regularly flush the lines with acid, judging exactly how much acid needed to be pushed in and pumped out so that it would not end up in her blood supply.

I was numb with shock as the nurses walked into Maya's hospital room. They wore plastic suits like those seen in the movies, decontamination suits in a futuristic nuclear war zone. The nurses put gloves on and protective eyewear, and whilst following a thorough procedure, they hooked Maya up to multiple lines that connected to a large double IV machine that monitored how fast the drugs went in. The lines had something like adaptors on them so that more and more lines could be added into the system. Here she was, a tiny eleven-month-old baby, hooked up to multiple lines. The amount of fluid that was pumped through her tiny body over the months caused her to become chubby due to fluid retention.

As part of Maya's protocol, she had chemotherapy once a month, which was given over five days; it consisted of four or more different drugs. The common ones were called bleomycin, etoposide, and cisplatin. The chemo drugs vincristine and doxorubicin were also occasionally used. The first drug that was given caused Maya to start vomiting within one to two minutes; we timed it. In fact, from the time she started treatment, Maya vomited continually, and over the months, the stomach acid left a red burn mark on her cheeks from when she vomited whilst laying on her side. Eventually, the acid wore the enamel off her teeth. Further, when this drug was being administered, the nurse would stand by the bed waiting. She watched the blood pressure monitor because this drug caused Maya's blood pressure to drop dramatically. When it started dropping, the nurse, Neil, and I quickly wound down the head of the bed so that Maya's feet were higher than her head. This caused the blood to rush to her brain and helped her avoid developing brain damage. As you can imagine, I earnestly uttered many prayers each time this occurred.

The offending drug was called amifostine and was used in conjunction with her primary chemo drug, cisplatin. After Maya's first course of chemo, Luc came to us and told us that the board of doctors had conducted discussions and decided that Maya's dose of cisplatin should be doubled. There had been a lot of success overseas when this was done. Even though the first dose had a very positive effect on Maya's cancer, shrinking it dramatically, they thought this was the best option. However, it came with a con: one in four people who had this double dose lost their hearing. This occurred even though amifostine was used to try to protect the ears from damage. We told Luc that we would prefer things to stay as they were. The chemo was working, and we wanted our little girl to keep her hearing; playing music to her had soothed her from her earliest days. After a day or so, Luc returned and told us that doing the double dose was what the doctors believed was best, so we agreed.

Not all of the drugs given to Maya had a negative effect on her. For all the damage done in the bid to eradicate the cancer cells, other drugs were given to counteract the damage. For example, Maya's protocol also involved the use of G-CSF (granulocyte colony-stimulating factor), which stimulated the production of neutrophils, a type of white blood cell produced in the bone marrow that responds to infection and attacks bacteria. Neutropenia is the term used when a patient has a weakened immune system due to a low level of neutrophils and is far more susceptible to infection and illness. Within a week of receiving chemotherapy, patients become neutropenic, and then their blood count begins to regain normality in time to be hit with chemotherapy again.

At the very beginning of Maya's treatment, she had her bone marrow harvested and placed on a shelf in case it was ever needed. When chemotherapy is as aggressive as Maya's was, it is not unusual for the chemo to destroy healthy bone marrow. Bone marrow transplants allow doctors to aggressively attack the cancer and replace the bone marrow afterward. However, in Maya's case, this was not needed, and the bone marrow is still sitting on a shelf in the hospital somewhere many years later.

In the first month or so, Maya was moved around wards, and, but for one night in Ronald McDonald House, remained an inhabitant of the hospital. The way we worked our sleeping arrangement meant that from the time of our arrival at the hospital, our family was separated each night. Neil and I took it in turns to stay with Maya, two nights on, two nights off. Whoever was staying at Ronald McDonald House looked after Emmy; whoever stayed at the hospital took care of Maya; and then we swapped after Maya had her breakfast in the morning. I got used to walking through the hospital in my pyjamas, seeing the massive hospital as my mansion and the hospital foyer as the front door where I farewelled our visitors before walking with bare feet back up to the ward. Our 'watch' involved feeding Maya the very little food that she ate; she had a nasogastric tube down her nose and she was given TPN (total parenteral nutrition), a liquid nutrition supplement. Ironically, Maya was given TPN because she could not eat or keep food down, yet the TPN caused her to vomit more. It was a constant battle keeping her bedding clean and keeping her weight up.

We were also responsible for doing catheterisations on Maya every three or four hours, even through the night, because her bladder was paralysed so she needed assistance. Because the nurses did so many catheterisations on so many people of all different shapes and sizes, Neil and I had more success at getting the tube in on the first go, which helped to avoid pain and discomfort for Maya.

One of the biggest shocks for me was lying on the little pull-out hospital bed beside Maya's bed and having people walking around whilst I slept, or tried to. It just seemed so bizarre. It was like having strangers walk into my bedroom at home and walk around tidying up while I slept. I have long said that if you need rest, do not go to a hospital to get it; they are the noisiest places on earth. Not only did Maya's IV machine alarm go off all night long, the electric pump that fed her the Pediasure, another liquid nutrition that eventually replaced the TPN, whirred all night. And in the distance, I could hear other patients' machines, as well as the sounds of patients' buzzers, telephones ringing at the nurses' station, and food carts being wheeled over joints in the hospital floor.

At first, things went along smoothly, well, as smoothly as one could hope for in such a situation. However, I recall being in Ronald McDonald House one afternoon, around two months into the battle, and Neil rang from the hospital. He explained that Maya was to be moved to another ward because routine blood tests showed that she had contracted the super bug MRSA. This is a staph infection that is resistant to antibiotics and, therefore, very dangerous for patients who are neutropenic, as Maya was every month after treatment. Maya was moved to 'Variety Ward', a ward sponsored by the charity Variety Club. This was an infectious disease ward. From then on, any objects that went into Maya's hospital room could not come back out without stringent procedures taken. Doctors and nurses used the same stethoscope that stayed in her room, hospital cutlery was changed to plastic cutlery, and everyone who entered her room had to wash and sanitise their hands and put on gowns and gloves. A routine trip to have testing done became a bigger ordeal; the orderly would be gowned, Maya's medical files were bagged and sealed, and when she got to the room for testing, every piece of machinery would be covered with a white sheet. Maya and another patient, Rachel, a fourteen-year-old girl with leukaemia, were the only two patients in the hospital with the virus. Even though it certainly had its downfalls, at least Maya was always promised her own room.

Unfortunately, towards the end of our stay at the hospital, Rachel, who had just finished her final course of treatment and was heading home for good, died as a result of the virus rearing its ugly head; within days, she was gone. I remember the nurses being very upset and continually asking us how we were coping with the news of Rachel's passing, not knowing yet the how or the why. We replied that it was tragic and we felt for the family, but I could not understand why they were so concerned about us. I was walking through 'my house' a little later and saw Luc in the corridor, and he explained that Rachel had died as a result of the virus. Then I understood why everyone was concerned about us. Maya was now the only patient in the hospital with the virus and could experience the same tragic outcome. Thankfully, by that time, Maya was finishing up her treatment and did not end up having any more chemo. This meant she would not be neutropenic again, and, therefore, susceptible. We experienced this and many more acts of God's grace during our time in the hospital.

Chapter Six

PEACE DURING THE BATTLE

Peace I leave with you, My peace I give to you;
not as the world gives do I give to you.
Let not your heart be troubled, neither let it be afraid

John 14:27 (New King James Version)

··•

The situation that our family found itself in was extremely stressful to say the very least. The busyness of hospital life helped keep us too busy to contemplate fully our dilemma. However, in the evenings when Neil and Emmy were down at the house and Maya was in her hospital bed asleep, I would lie on the pull-out bed looking out over the city lights of Sydney and shed tears. It was really the only time that I allowed myself to become overwhelmed. It is difficult to explain the way that I coped, but I can say that it was certainly a one-day-at-a-time journey. I know with absolute certainty what it is like to rely completely on God. In my quiet moments of reflection, it was not hard to see that even though we still had Maya with us, we had lost so much. All of our possessions were locked away in a shed over four hours away; I missed our beloved dog; we had to eventually give up the church when we realised that Maya would need ongoing medical attention even when she was cured of cancer, so living in a regional town was not an option; and I was far from my friends and family. I did grieve for what we had lost in just having a normal life, with a healthy child who did everything within expected developmental stages. I also missed silly things like my own ironing board. The first time we went to the local supermarket, I was affronted by the realisation that, despite our ordeal with our daughter's cancer battle, life went on as normal for everyone else. I remember feeling like I wanted to shout out in the supermarket, 'Don't you understand what we are dealing with?'

Despite the battle that raged, I felt a peace that defied explanation, and I knew what was meant by the scripture in Philippians 4:6-7, which states, 'Be anxious for nothing, but in everything by prayer and supplication, with thanksgiving, let your requests be made known to God; and the peace of God, which surpasses all understanding, will guard your hearts and minds through Christ Jesus.' (NKJV)

I remember telling the state chairman of our denomination early on in the battle that I felt quite at peace, and I was not yet sure if it was the peace spoken about in Philippians 4:6-7 or whether I was simply in denial. As it turned out, it was the former, not the latter. I know for certain that the experiences that I had as a child, and the protection that I received from God at the time, provided me with the strength, trust, and faith that I needed to get through every day. I figured that if God had gone to so much trouble to protect me and keep me in my youth, He would certainly continue even in the midst of what I was now facing. At a young age, I had felt God so near me, and His presence in my life never left me, despite the circumstances.

Looking back, I realise there were many times when God intervened on our behalf so that Maya stayed with us. I clearly remember sitting in the hospital room with Neil's family on a sunny day, a few months into our ordeal, watching the nurse connect up the chemo drugs for that month's treatment. As I watched him, the words 'ask him which drug he is putting in' came to mind. I thought this was bizarre, but I asked the question. He told me the name of the drug, and immediately alarm bells sounded within me; he was about to make a huge mistake with regards to the strict sequence that the drugs should be put in. I kindly told him which drug he was supposed to put in, and after going away and checking, he came back and apologised and made the necessary changes. Similar situations occurred over the time spent in hospital; sometimes it came down to whether Maya would still be with us the next day.

On one occasion, late one evening, Maya was not herself. She grunted, shook, and seemed to be in a lot of pain. I felt an inner urgency to pursue it with the nurse. However, it was a weekend, and on weekends, Maya had agency nurses who did not see her regularly enough to know her well. The nurse came and assessed her and told me that she seemed okay and that her symptoms were nothing out of the ordinary, considering her illness. Rather than accepting this, I asked for the doctor on call to come and see her. When he did come and assess her, he organised a mobile X-ray machine to come up onto the ward to do an emergency X-ray of her abdomen. As it turned out, Maya was suffering from a near-perforated bowel. Had it burst, which it would have done within hours, the septic fluids would certainly have caused considerable damage, if not death, particularly as a result of her neutropenic state.

God's hand of protection even extended to outside of the hospital. I have always been a walker, and I have found that spending time in prayer and worship whilst enjoying the beauty of God's creation has provided me with the strength, peace, and communication with God that I have desperately needed throughout my life. I can honestly say that without these times of refreshment whilst Maya was in hospital, I would never have gotten through the battle. All people facing major battles can only do so in their own strength for so long before they have to rely on something bigger than themselves. My God and my Saviour was the safe refuge and the tower of strength that I needed at this and other very dark times.

So, one of my coping mechanisms was to listen to worship music whilst walking around the beautiful Parramatta Park situated on the Parramatta River near the hospital. I would rise early in the morning in the hospital and change before going for my walk. My eagerness, despite our trials, astounded the nurses who worked on the ward.

Little did they know it was the only thing keeping me sane!

With regards to God's protection, I had felt very strongly, for no particular reason, that I should not go walking in the park at that time. I had an uneasiness every time that I considered going for a walk, which I had done almost daily for months. As a result of my ill feeling, I decided to stop walking. A week later, a friend visiting us in hospital, who was a local, told me that a young lady had been attacked in an isolated part of the park in the week that I chose not to walk. Just as when I was young, the evidence of God's love and protection were a tangible part of my life and acted like an oasis in the desert to me. God's faithfulness towards me resounded louder than any negative report or difficult situation that I ever faced.

Sometime early in our stay at the hospital I felt led to make a commitment to God that regardless of whether Maya lived or died, I was not going to turn my back on Him. His faithfulness towards me throughout my life would not and could not allow me to turn my back upon such a loving, caring, steadfast God. As always, He was the one constant that I could always put my trust in. I recognised the peace that came from knowing God in a way that girded even the most troubled heart, and believe me, I had ample reasons to have a troubled heart.

Throughout the battle, not only was I dealing with Maya's illness and all of the stresses relating to that, but our marriage came under incredible attack. In looking back at our experience and observing the relationships of other couples at the hospital, it seems that overwhelming stresses, such as those we experienced, put a huge emotional burden on marriage relationships. Partners either come together to battle in one accord or pull apart and deal with the ordeal in different ways on their own. In our case, unfortunately, it was the latter. In our time at the hospital, Neil struggled greatly as the helpless father who could do very little to protect his daughter from the suffering she was experiencing. He chose to withdraw from me, and as a result, for a large part of the journey, we each did it alone. With the remaining strength that I had, which was not much, I worked diligently to try to keep our marriage healthy under such stressful circumstances.

As a result of this, and along with the rest of the intricacies of my situation, I found myself in a very, very dark place. Isolation is difficult at the best of times, but when you have lost everything and the ground continually shifts beneath you, it is a very desolate place to be. There is a place where one stands emotionally on the edge of a cliff, where even the slightest breeze would cause a fall over the edge into an abyss; I was in that place. I know what it is like to *see* darkness and *feel* darkness and to hold onto my sanity and sense of being with the last ounce of strength and resolution left. At these times, as in all other times, I cried out to the God who constantly saved me. In one of those dark times, when my whole life and everything I knew was under attack, I went for a walk around the park, listening to worship music. I remember being overwhelmed by Maya's illness, my threatened marriage, and my current lot in life, when a young man, out exercising, ran towards me. As he went by me, I heard him yell out to me, 'Smile! Surely it cannot be that bad!' All I wanted to do was turn around and yell at him what I was living with daily, but instead I watched him run off obliviously, without a care. Despite the trials that the young man was unaware of, I still held on to what I knew to be true. I refused to let go of the hope that I had in my God. I knew that God's love and faithfulness would endure regardless of the storm that raged. I have long said that our circumstances are temporary and do not determine who we are or who God is.

Chapter Seven

THE BATTLE IS WON

God's way is perfect.
All the LORD's promises prove true.
He is a shield for all who look to Him for protection

Psalm 18:30 (NLT)

....●

Maya was admitted to The Children's Hospital at Westmead on 23 January 2001, and she was discharged seven months later on 22 August 2001. After enduring a roller coaster ride of emotions and having battled against all the odds, we were at the end of the journey, having succeeded in the battle of keeping our little girl with us. By God's grace and by His power, she endured the treatment, recovered from any complications, and began to develop and grow. The cancer was finally gone. The chemotherapy had shrunken the mass down considerably, and then, on 2 July 2001 and 9 August 2001, Maya had surgery to remove the residual cancer and completely remove any traces of the dead cells. The surgeries left her with a very mutilated backside, but she was still with us and we were grateful.

As the chemo was given to Maya over the months, the cancer had disappeared from her spine and, as a result, her bladder recovered full function, and she regained the use of her right leg. However, she was left with permanent spinal damage, having no ability to move her toes or properly control her right foot. Further, partway through her treatment, Maya had a series of hearing tests which uncovered that she had, in fact, lost her hearing because of the double dose of cisplatin. She was severely deaf, one step down from profound hearing loss; she could hear nothing but the sound of a slamming door. When the hearing loss was first suspected, I would sneak into the hospital room whilst Maya was not looking and make a series of loud noises to see if she could hear me. She was always so excited to see us re-enter the room, so when she did not turn and respond, my worst fears were confirmed. However, again, she was still with us and that was all that mattered.

Oh, glorious day, when the central line was removed and the doctor signed off on Maya's paperwork with the comment 'CCC-Cute, Cancer, Cured'. We packed up our belongings, which had accumulated over the months, and said our tearful goodbyes to our beloved nurses, who we had gotten to know so well, and to the staff and other families in Ronald McDonald House, who were left to battle on without us. We had decided to do a tour to thank all of our loyal supporters, allowing them the opportunity to see the miracle bub they had prayed for, before settling in the Redlands region of Brisbane, Queensland, where Neil's brother, Wayne, and his wife, Kathy, were the senior pastors of the Christian Outreach Centre church in Cleveland. There was no chance of returning to pastor the church at Wellington as Maya still required a great deal of medical support, and rather than living in the huge, busy metropolis of Sydney, we thought we would settle in the more laid-back, bayside shire of Redlands, only a thirty-minute drive from the CBD of Brisbane. We made arrangements for the hospital in Brisbane to take over Maya's care, monitoring her and testing her blood to ensure that the cancer was not coming back. We said goodbye to our beloved oncologist, Luc, who told us that Maya's cancer was very aggressive, and if it did not come back in the first year and a half, she would be completely free of it.

I will never forget the day we bundled Maya into the car, with Emmy, and drove away from the hospital. It was a beautiful day with a blue sky. We were heading to Wellington so that our church members could see Maya and we could say goodbye as we headed north and interstate. The next part of the tour involved going home to Taree where Neil's parents threw a 'miracle party' on their farm, which was a huge celebration that even my elderly and frail nan attended. As we left Sydney on that auspicious day, the U2 song 'Beautiful Day' came on the radio. Despite all that we had been through in the last seven or so months, that was the only time that I cried in front of Neil and the girls. We had survived the battle, all of us. The lyrics in the song perfectly summed up our lives and how I felt at that very moment. Not only had we survived to see a beautiful day, but the lyrics also spoke of there being no place for us, of being stuck somewhere and not being able to move, of having no destination, and of having life take over us, and yet . . . and yet, God had made everything beautiful in its time (Ecclesiastes 3:11).

We eventually arrived in Brisbane, and our move to Queensland signalled a new beginning for us; it was refreshing and novel to have our little family together under one roof. We stayed with Wayne and Kath until we found a rental property. We visited the hospital that was now responsible for Maya's care, The Royal Children's Hospital in Herston, Brisbane. We met Maya's new oncologist, who was to monitor her test results. A simple monthly blood test would tell us if the cancer was coming back. Also, within weeks, Maya was receiving considerable medical attention from most departments within the hospital. She was allocated a physiotherapist to help her to start walking; an occupational therapist; a speech therapist; a dietician; an orthopaedic surgeon to deal with her leg and foot; a kidney doctor to monitor her kidney function; an ear, nose and throat doctor for her hearing; a social worker to help us with any needed support; as well as external support with a government hearing service called Australian Hearing, which issued Maya with her first hearing aids. Eventually, she became a client at St Gabriel's School for Hearing Impaired Children, attending weekly speech appointments in South Brisbane, just a stone's throw from Brisbane's iconic riverside, man-made beach, South Bank, and its nearby arts precinct. We were worlds away from the seemingly limitless red soil paddocks of Wee Waa and the everybody-knows-your-name small town of Wellington.

As we had suspected in the beginning when we gave up pastoring the church, Maya needed a lot of care and rehabilitation. For the first four years of our time in Brisbane, Maya and I attended nine appointments a week, mostly of a medical nature, whilst Emmy resumed the normal life of a student at school.

When we arrived in Brisbane, Maya was one year and seven months old. After being strapped into a special standing frame called a Jenx Monkey Stander for multiple hours a day, which was used to strengthened the bones and muscles in her legs, she finally began walking at the age of two and a half.

In other areas of her life, she made gradual progress. Part of the reason for her delayed development could be attributed to her less-than-normal start in life. She had not had the same opportunities to explore and play as other children; instead, she had lived in a small hospital room with a little window. It also didn't help that Maya had so many appointments to go to once we were in Brisbane. If we were not in an appointment, we were driving to or from one. Therefore, when Maya was old enough to go to Grade One at school in a little blue uniform, wearing hearing aids on both ears and a plastic orthopaedic splint on her right leg, I vowed that she would begin to live as normal a life as possible. I contacted all of the medical support services, which had doubled over time, to tell them that unless it was utterly necessary, Maya would not be attending any appointments.

The reason the medical support had increased was that Maya had begun being supported by another hospital, The Mater Children's Hospital in South Brisbane, because we sought a second opinion with regards to the paralysis in her right leg. Her original doctor wanted to wait until she was eight years old before doing any surgical interventions on her leg to help her walk better. As a result of having little or no control over her foot and toes, she walked on the outer side of her foot only, which had started to form calluses.

Further, and more importantly, we were concerned that walking in such a way for approximately another three years would make her gait very difficult to correct. The splint helped to keep all of her muscles stretched and pliable, forcing the leg into a correct position, but without it she walked in this awkward way. We ended up connecting with an amazing orthopaedic surgeon named Dr Terence McGuire, an elderly man with a wealth of knowledge. He videoed Maya walking in the very first appointment, and from then on, he was determined to see her walk properly. That first appointment with him gave us incredible hope. Over the years, Dr McGuire constantly referred to that video, amazed, himself, at her progress. On top of the three operations and other procedures that Maya had whilst in hospital in Sydney, she went on, in the following years in Brisbane, to have two operations on her leg and foot to correct her gait, the first on the 16 August 2004 and the second on 28 August 2006. These operations involved doing tendon transfers to bring more control to her foot in the weaker, non-functioning areas.

In addition, in the same year as the latter leg operation, Maya had the first of two Cochlear ear implant operations on 3 April. The second was on 6 December 2010. Her hearing had depreciated so much over the previous few years that she heard very little with the hearing aids and needed further assistance. Even though the battle for survival against cancer had been won, a battle still raged. The support of family, friends, and our church was amazing, and, as always, and expectedly, God was my continual source of strength and peace.

From the time when Maya was required to have routine blood tests to see if the cancer was coming back, I felt an incredible peace, like the peace I had experienced in Sydney. The days of waiting for the results to come back were never underpinned with concern or fretting. The thing was, I knew in my heart and my spirit that God was not going to allow me to go through that battle again with Maya. It was an unsaid agreement between God and me; we both knew that I did not have the ability to do that battle with her again. Scripture says that God does not allow us to go through more than we can handle (1 Corinthians 10:13), and I just knew that the battle for Maya was over because I had given everything that I had. The only time that I became alarmed over a blood test result occurred only a month or so after arriving in Brisbane.

With the type of cancer Maya battled, it was easy to detect its development by checking a particular protein in the blood, the alphafetoprotein level, also known as the AFP. When Maya was first diagnosed, Luc knew that Maya's body was riddled with cancer because the AFP count was something like 130 million, whereas a healthy person's count is not above six. Yes, a single digit number. I still remember standing in front of the church and giving a testimony shortly after we arrived in Brisbane: Maya's AFP count had gone down to 5. She continued having blood tests for the first year, but then even that was abandoned.

However, there was the one instance of alarm when, for some reason, Maya's AFP level skyrocketed overnight. I called Luc on the phone in a panic, and he gave some alternative reasons for why this could be so. His reasoning ended up being true; it was simply the consequence of a bowel complication. However, whilst we waited to find out whether or not the cancer was indeed coming back, I had another spiritual epiphany. My God had gotten me through so much that if it was coming back, I would simply have to trust God again. The scripture that became my adage at that time and has stayed close to my heart ever since is found in the book of Job, where God's servant Job finds out that he has lost most of his family, as well as his possessions, in tragic circumstances. It says:

Then Job arose, tore his robe, and shaved his head; and he fell to the ground and worshiped. And he said: 'Naked I came from my mother's womb, And naked shall I return there.

The LORD gave, and the LORD has taken away; Blessed be the name of the LORD.'

–Job 1:20-21 (NKJV)

That was the scripture that I chose to live by. No matter what happened, no matter what I lost, I would still say, 'Blessed be the name of the Lord.' That philosophy would stand me in good stead in years to come. Again, little did I know what the future held for me.

Chapter Eight

A LAND OF MILK AND HONEY

So I have come down to deliver them out of the hand of the Egyptians, and to bring them up from that land to a good and large land, to a land flowing with milk and honey

Exodus 3:8 (NKJV)

....●

Not only did the scripture in Job resonate with me, but Job's whole story in the Bible seemed to mirror my own.

I had been through an experience where I felt like I had lost everything, now here we were in the Israelites' land of milk and honey, enjoying a new life. I felt that, as in Job's story, everything was returned to us one hundredfold. Within a year of being in Brisbane, Neil bought a garden bag business from a family friend, which involved Neil taking away customers' green waste every month. Over time, the business grew as we advertised and bought clientele from other businesses. Not only did it provide for us financially, but the business became a mission-field opportunity for Neil, who loved to talk with and minister to his customers, approximately six hundred across the city. I managed the home, looked after the girls, and did all the paperwork for the business.

Life was good; we had normality. Eventually, on 6 September 2003, we were blessed with the final addition to our family, another daughter, Callie Mae. She completed the hundredfold return, being a healthy, beautiful girl who met all the developmental benchmarks at the right times. Emmy and Maya were mirror images of their mother, but Callie came out of the womb looking like her father. She was tall and lanky at birth and had her dad's facial features and mousy-brown hair. Excepting the usual pressures that most couples and families face at times, we were settled, happy, and living in God's blessings, having moved into our own home four months before Callie was born.

Being in this environment of blessing and opportunity, I started to dream. As a young child, I had pretended to be a school teacher, forcing my sister and brothers to sit quietly while I taught them geography using a world map hanging on the wall. I had always been fascinated by the acquisition of weird and wonderful facts, such as information about tree kangaroos and the longest earth worms on the planet. Throughout my schooling, I had been very successful in academic pursuits, being selected for spelling bee competitions in primary school and usually sitting in the top percentage of the class or coming first in the year level in high school. This was despite my receiving no encouragement at all from home to do well in school or even attend.

My academic interests were balanced by a love of the arts. I was enamoured with poetry, classic novels, and classical music. When most teenage girls were off chasing teenage boys, I was shut up in my room listening to Richard Clayderman playing instrumental piano or Kenny G playing the saxophone. I had an old record player and had been given some records of classical movie soundtracks; my favourite piece was 'The March of the Siamese Children' from *The King and I*. I would sit for hours listening to music whilst writing poetry about God or reading through books on roses, admiring their beauty and learning about their genealogy and taking notes. Yes, I was a little weird and certainly did not fit into the environment that I had been born into. The most salient special memories are of me performing a monologue on stage in church when I was primary-school-aged, citing from memory; writing multiple plays to be performed in puppet shows in church when I was in my early teens, supported greatly by Alice Mitchison; and writing and directing a play about the rapture in 1992 when I was seventeen, approximately three years before the first book in the *Left Behind* series was published. It was a huge production that packed the church, with an overflow of people standing up the back of the large auditorium.

As a result of all these personal loves and interests, I had often wished that I had become a teacher, but with a family who was barely literate, where nobody had finished high school let alone attended university, it was something that I had not thought possible. It was completely out of reach. However, in 2006, the desire to go to university and become a teacher grew. One day, when I walked into a Post Shop and saw a fridge magnet with the words 'life is not a dress rehearsal', I decided to take the leap and put action to my dreams. It didn't hurt that Anne Shirley was a teacher, too. Neil supported me in my goal, and in June 2006, I attended TAFE to polish up on my academic skills, which had lain dormant for some time. I did well at TAFE, extremely well, in fact. So much so that in sitting a three-hour senior mathematics exam on geometry and trigonometry, I got 100 percent correct. I continued in my pursuit to go to university by sitting a tertiary entrance exam. I sat in the large lecture hall with hundreds of other participants, and towards the end of the allocated time I noticed that many people had finished, sitting with their pens on the desks. I did not finish the exam paper, leaving approximately ten questions unanswered. I thought to myself as I left, 'Oh, well. I must not have done too well with that'. Weeks later, I came home from TAFE for lunch to see the results letter in the mailbox. I opened it to find that I had done much better than I had expected. In fact, when looking at the percentages across both literacy and numeracy, if I were in a room with ninety-nine other people, only ten of them would have done better on the exam than I had. In that moment, with tears in my eyes, I prayed to God and humbly dedicated to Him the gift that He had given me and told Him that I would use it to honour Him in whatever way He led me.

I applied to two universities and accepted a place at a smaller Christian college called Christian Heritage College (CHC), located in Carindale, Brisbane, where I started my degree, a bachelor of arts and a bachelor of education, to become a secondary teacher specialising in the two teaching areas of English and History. From the beginning of my time at CHC, I did quite well academically, receiving the highest possible marks across all subjects for the majority of my time there. I enjoyed learning about learning and enjoyed, more so, hanging out with the other students, some of who would become lifelong friends. My time at CHC began a journey of self-discovery and transformation, underpinned by the stress of being a uni student. Yet, that stress was only a blip on the radar compared with the stress that was to come.

Chapter Nine

A RETURN TO BATTLE

God is our refuge and strength,
a very present help in trouble

Psalm 46:1 (NKJV)

....●

idway through 2007, when I was in my first semester at
CHC, Neil noticed a little lump on the right side of his
neck. We were not too concerned in the beginning; well,
we tried not to be. Neil went to the local general practitioner, and
the doctor began to do a series of tests. However, the test results did
not really reveal anything. Months passed, and every now and then,
when looking at Neil, I would see it there on the side of his neck. I
tried hard not to panic, and as before in a very, very similar situation,
I chose to trust the process of medical testing. Eventually, after three
or so months of trying to convince my laid-back husband to push for
more answers, I called his GP. In the course of the conversation with
the doctor, I explained that I was getting exasperated. The doctor
had even tested for cat scratch disease, a benign infectious disease
that resulted from a scratch or bite from a cat. I told the doctor in
an incredulous tone that Neil hated cats with a vengeance and never
went near them. I went on to tell him about Maya and that I was

finding myself in a familiar place to where I had been with her. He responded by saying, 'If you are not happy with the level of care your husband is receiving, you need to contact your local member for parliament.' Well, that did not sit well! I told the doctor that he should just biopsy the site, which was something he considered doing in the beginning. Instead, after hanging up, he passed on Neil's case to a specialist, who was happy to help out.

Within a week of Neil going for tests, the specialist called us and asked us to come see him the next day. He went on to explain that some of the results had returned and they showed evidence of the presence of cancer. He said he would have more information for us when we saw him. I do not remember much of what happened that day, but I do recall sitting in a lounge chair whilst the girls played around me, staring into space and struggling to keep control of my thoughts and emotions. We had a family friend staying with us at the time, and he told me not to worry unnecessarily and prematurely. However, that one word 'cancer' had a thunderous effect on me. To go through a battle with cancer for the first time was a lot different to going through a battle with cancer knowing exactly what I was going to face.

Of course, Neil was also greatly affected by the news; he began looking on the Internet for cancers that presented as lumps on the neck. He discovered that lymphoma, a type of cancer that attacks the lymph glands, presented in a similar way; the prognosis was generally good and there was a reasonably high success rate for survival. The next day, Neil and I made our way to the specialist's office. It was late afternoon on 27 September 2007. The girls were at home with our family friend and had no idea of the situation.

We hesitantly sat down in chairs in front of the doctor's desk. He told us with no ceremony that Neil had lung cancer. As a non-smoker, it was a one-in-four-million chance of getting it. Due to it metastasising in the lymph glands, it was terminal. He went on to say that with treatment, Neil would probably live twelve months, without, maybe six. Whilst we sat there in complete and utter shock, the doctor went on to ask questions that no doctor should ask in such a situation. He asked, 'Do you have children?' and 'How old are they?' Neil broke down in tears, and I, also in tears, managed to utter the information he sought and then told him that they were not good questions to ask right then.

The doctor was lovely; I could see that giving such bad news affected him. He waived his consultation fee, and we walked out the door. Once we were out of view of the doctor, I completely broke down, and Neil put his arm around me. I could not face going home, so I asked Neil if we could drive somewhere and park. He stopped at a local store to buy us bottled drinks, and then we drove down to Cleveland Point, overlooking Moreton Bay. Many times since, when walking past that little store where Neil bought the drinks, I have wondered what was going through his head in that moment. I know that as I waited in the car with my window wound down, I was taking deep breaths of fresh air and thinking that that was something Neil would not be able to do soon.

Down at the Point, Neil and I discussed through tears what we were feeling. In the shock of the news, all faith had left me; I was completely overwhelmed. I remember telling Neil that he could not go anywhere. He was the 'fun' parent; I could not do it without him. After some time, whilst I sat in the passenger seat, Neil rang his parents and told his mum the news. Sitting next to Neil, I could clearly hear her response of utter despair as she cried into the phone. A new wave of emotion swept over me: Could this really be happening again?

After an hour or so, I still did not want to go home. I did not want to alarm the girls, but I could not pull myself together. However, we could not stay down at the Point forever; we had to face what was ahead. Quietly, we drove home. I steadied myself as best I could and walked in the door of our home. Neil's sister, Loren, was already there, having been rung by her parents. Without saying a word, I made my way towards the bedroom. Our family friend put out his arms to give me a hug and all I could manage to do was put my hand up to say a silent 'No.'

Once behind the closed door of our bedroom, I lost all ability to compose myself. With my head in my hands, doubled over with what was like a physical pain, I suffered a panic attack. I knew what was coming. How could this happen again? Where was God in this? At this time, Neil was outside in the yard near our bedroom window. I overheard him talking on the phone, with all the courage he could muster, to his brother, Wayne, who was on a mission trip in Malaysia at the time. That night is a bit of a blur to me now, but I do recall calling my best friend, Joanne in Narrabri, to tell her the news. She was in shock and asked, 'Why does this always happen to you?' She then went on to say what I had expected she would say before I even made the call: 'Well, we will just do it all again!' She went on to alert our friends the Pattisons. A similar call was made to my family, who offered their support. I made a final call to another close friend, Ronda Gladwell. She and her husband, Paddy, were very good friends of ours, and their support became pivotal to me in the coming months and years. Due to my call with Ronda, faith began to rise within me. I would, again, believe God would save us, protect us, and get us out of the mess we were in. I communicated this to Neil, and we both agreed to trust God throughout the new battle.

In the beginning, we decided not to tell the girls. However, with continual phone calls coming into the house where we had to leave the room to talk openly, as well as the added tension, it was obvious to Emmy that something was going on. At some point early on, we sat the three girls down and told them, 'Dad is sick, but he will be okay. Do not worry'. At the time, Emmy was nine years old, Maya was seven, and Callie had just turned four.

The first time we went to meet with the oncologist that Neil had been allocated, a lovely, attractive woman called Dr Kath Shannon, I said to Neil, 'Now remember, it doesn't matter what they say in that room. None of them created the universe. Just remember that'. From the beginning, I refused to believe any negative reports. I chose to have faith and believe what was said in the Bible about God's healing power. Neil would be healed. I did not know when or how, but he would.

Neil was to have eleven doses of chemotherapy over

approximately four months, and guess what? The chemo drug of choice was cisplatin, the drug that damaged Maya's hearing. We were to meet with Dr Shannon before going up to the Oncology Day Ward of the Mater Adult Hospital in South Brisbane, next to the children's hospital where Maya had her leg surgeries. The Oncology Day Ward would be where Neil would have the chemotherapy treatment. At the start of the battle, Neil was very upbeat and was his usual 'exasperating' self. This is what Dr Shannon called him because he constantly baited her for reactions whilst she tried to act serious. He displayed a cheeky smile while he did it. In fact, Neil became a favourite with all the nurses, doctors, and administration staff, which was no surprise; he had been a favourite at The Children's Hospital at Westmead in Sydney, also. On one occasion there, Maya had a young nurse, Rebecca, who was quite short-tempered. If we asked her for anything, she obliged with an air of dissatisfaction. So, one day, whilst Rebecca was getting something out of a large linen cupboard, Neil pushed her in and closed the door. She came out all flustered, trying to appear angered, but the smile on her face gave her away; they were best friends after that.

On our first visit to the oncology ward for Neil's treatment, I was shocked to see just how many people battled with this deadly disease. There were numerous large rooms situated down the length of the ward. In each of these large rooms there were recliner chairs lined up on both sides of the room, six or so, with a little table beside and a curtain hanging from the ceiling to provide privacy if it was needed. I likened the rooms to cattle stalls, and every chair was taken with an adult who was hooked up to machines pumping chemicals into his or her body. The nurses were there with their familiar protective wear, and the common procedures that took place reminded us of another time. We were both apprehensive yet positive on that first visit. I even took photos of Neil having his first course of chemotherapy on 17 October 2007 while, ever the trickster and clown, he posed in the photo as if he were deathly ill and on his last legs.

Unfortunately, Neil did not cope very well with the chemotherapy. Like Maya, he vomited continually. Being tall and lanky as he was, it was not like he could afford to be bringing up his food all the time. Over the course of the treatment, the nurses tried everything that they could think of to stop him from vomiting. I even brought along my laptop with DVDs to try to distract him, but that did little to help. As the months went on, he vomited before he even left home to go to the hospital; it had become a problem that was triggered whenever he thought of treatment. In the end, the nurses gave him sedatives and the anti–nausea medication, ondansetron, to take at home on the morning of treatment before he left for the hospital; this only made it slightly better. After the day's course of treatment, I would drive him home, trying not to make sudden turns or stop too quickly. Many times, he vomited into a bag whilst I drove.

Incredibly, for the four months of chemotherapy treatment, Neil's brother, Wayne, and some of Neil's best friends, of which he had many, volunteered to work the business for us, picking up garden bags. Some even travelled from interstate to help. Unfortunately, it was over the summer months, and they all looked dirty and exhausted when they came home to drop off the truck for the next poor volunteer.

With regards to my college degree, I took it one semester at a time. A pattern seemed to emerge over the months of Neil's treatment around the holidays. He was diagnosed in the September school holidays, and we seemed to always see his oncologist, Dr Shannon, during the school holidays, which aligned with my college breaks. Each time, I would leave the doctor's office with the okay to go back to college for the next semester because things were stable and the chemotherapy was shrinking the cancer. I recall one time the doctor's appointment was on the first day of my college semester. When I got the okay from the doctor, I asked Neil to quickly drop me off at the college. I made it to my first class with minutes to spare, having no pens or books. This was how it went for the first half of my four years at college. Despite Neil's battle, he was adamant that I would continue in my pursuit of gaining my teaching degree. I even typed up assignments while sitting in the oncology ward while Neil had his treatment, and somehow, by God's grace, I still managed to receive top marks.

Every month, during treatment, Neil had a CT scan to see what was happening with the cancer, and every time, we sat quietly as we opened the results. Unfortunately, each time it stated that even though the cancer had decreased in size, it was still there. Towards the end of the four months of treatment, we made the best of Christmas 2007, staying on the Tyrie family farm in Lansdowne and catching up with my family. Neil was still ill from chemotherapy and spent a lot of time sleeping. All the while, the family and I hoped and prayed to God that we would all be together for the next Christmas.

On 30 January 2008, Neil had his last dose of chemotherapy and it looked like there was a possibility that only scar tissue remained; 'Maybe,' said the doctor. Then the doctor said, 'That is it'; the treatment was finished and the waiting game began. This created panic in me; we were being let loose in the world to see what would happen.

In February, we went on a short family holiday with our good friends, the Day family: Craig and Sue, and their beautiful children, Gemmanda, Ashleigh and Harrison. We stayed in the breathtaking Bunyah Mountains and enjoyed our time together. Neil was hesitant to go at first, but I insisted; we deserved a holiday together as a family after all that we had been through in the previous six months or so. I am forever grateful that we did go because some of our most treasured photos were taken on that trip, including photos of Neil moving a snake off a bush trail. Playing with snakes, both venomous and non-venomous, had been his favourite pastime in his youth. My favourite photos, though, are the ones where Neil was walking down a bush track with his girls, Maya and Callie. The girls, dressed in shades of pink, did not have a care in the world as they walked with their dad. The photos of Neil having a grass fight with Emmy, Maya, and Callie also rate highly as treasured photos in our collection.

After treatment, Neil went back to working the business, and for the next nine months, things were fairly normal. I continued on at college and even went away out west to Dalby by myself for four weeks to do a practicum for teaching, travelling home on weekends.

It seemed that life had taken a turn for the better; God had protected us through such a difficult time. I recall telling someone how blessed I felt at that time because the difficult times made me appreciate more what I had, and I saw the best in everything. Even flowers looked more beautiful. Going through such difficult times as I had, I did not sweat the small stuff; I had seen enough of God's favour on us to know that He had things under control. Our gratefulness to God for his saving grace was immeasurable. We saw His hand in everything, His love, His protection, His strength. However, what we had faced in the last year and a half was, again, just a drop in the bucket compared to what was in store for us.

Chapter Ten

THE VALLEY OF THE
SHADOW OF DEATH

*Yea, though I walk through the valley of the
shadow of death, I will fear no evil;
For You are with me;
Your rod and Your staff, they comfort me'*

Psalm 23:4 (NKJV)

A gain it was the school holidays, spanning September into October of 2008. Neil had been off treatment for nine months, and we were camping up the coast at a little seaside town called Poona. We had camped a few times over the years, enjoying family time whilst fishing, swimming and eating lots of food. However, this trip was dampened by the realisation that the lymph glands on the right side of Neil's neck had become quite swollen in the preceding weeks. We did not talk about it much. I prayed a lot and told myself that it was a result of excess lymphatic fluid, which had previously presented under his armpit and down his arm. I remember Neil and I stood by the water at night looking up at the stars while Neil held a fishing rod. It was serene and beautiful, and I wondered many times later on what it was that Neil was thinking in that moment where creation was so beautifully on display and one could sense the majesty of the One who had created it. I daresay that he was confiding in his God all the concerns and fears that he was feeling at that time.

In early December 2008, Neil got quite ill; he was vomiting a lot. He had a sore tooth, which we suspected was infected, so I hoped that his symptoms were simply a result of the infection. He had it pulled out and was given antibiotics to take. We then packed up our belongings to head down to the farm for Christmas. Yes, it was the holidays. I should have known. Neil drove the girls and I the nine-hour trip down, towing his boat, which he planned on using. I think he suspected that it might be his last chance to do so. We arrived in the evening at Neil's parents' home, which had also been my 'home' for the thirteen and a half years of our marriage. The next evening, we went to dinner at a new eatery in the new roadside service centre, catching up with my mum; my sister, Monika; her husband, Trevor; and their two beautiful girls, Aliesha and Jayde. All was great. Neil was chatting with us all, and then he went to the toilet in the complex. He seemed to take a long time, and when he did emerge, he wandered around with a puzzled look on his face, staring at the signs. We watched him and lightly joked that he looked like he was lost. Emmy went over to him, and together they walked back to the table to join us. When he was asked why he was wandering around, he said he was confused and did not know where he was. Instantly, I became alarmed. I decided it was time to go, and we headed towards the car. We did not make it; Neil started vomiting in the garden. I began to panic and told him we were going to the hospital to get a check-up. He had no intention of going, so I called for reinforcements—his mum. She told me to take him to the hospital anyway. My sister met us at the hospital and offered to take the girls home with her, which helped a lot. Cancer patients get priority in the Emergency Department, so, within a short time, Neil was in a hospital bed being kept in overnight for observation and for testing in the morning. The staff said his oncologist would be contacted for guidance. Because there was no bed for me, or even a padded chair, I left Neil there and went home to the farm to return again in the morning.

The next day, sitting with Neil, I explained to the doctors that Neil had suffered recently from a bad tooth and that his current symptoms were likely a result of that; I refused to believe anything else. I told Neil this and then he admitted to me that he had had similar episodes of confusion when he was at home in Brisbane. He would be driving the work truck and would need to pull over due to not knowing where he was. A week or so before we headed south for Christmas, it had happened when he had driven into the city with Maya for an event held for children with special needs.

My belief in a favourable cause was dashed into oblivion when the doctor came into the room and told us that the results showed that the cancer had spread into Neil's brain and was quite substantial, so much so that he had experienced a midline shift; the line down the centre of his brain was no longer down the middle, but had been pushed over by the tumour. This accounted for the episodes of confusion and the vomiting. As one can imagine, this news was extremely difficult to take in. However, as always, I chose to believe that we were in the palm of God's hand and that He would save us from this dark and difficult situation. I left the hospital on that beautiful, sunny December day to get the car so I could pick up Neil, thinking, as I walked, that things had changed forever. I had no idea what was ahead of us except that Dr Shannon had rung and said that Neil should return home early; she wanted to discuss the option of radiation with us. So, we travelled silently back to the family farm to try, as best we could, to enjoy Christmas with our girls and the family. It was 23 December 2008, two days before Christmas.

We made the best of Christmas, not telling the girls the news. We wanted them to have a carefree holiday. They had already watched their dad battle cancer for one year and three months, seeing him vomiting continually, struggling to walk at times, and sleeping a lot. They would find out all too soon, so why rush it? We organised for Neil's parents to keep the girls on the farm while we travelled back to see Dr Shannon. That nine-hour trip back to Brisbane will always stay in my memory as a treasured time that Neil and I spent together on our own. Due to the cancer metastasising to Neil's brain, I had to drive because he was not allowed to. I towed the boat that never got used, and we talked of many things, but not necessarily our new predicament. We held hands as we walked to get lunch, and Neil talked about a song that was playing on the Christian radio station that meant a lot to him at the time. He also mentioned how proud he was of Emmy for liking another song that played, which spoke of seeing the pain in others. We just tried to enjoy the time we had together. However, this was interrupted by the occasional reference to his new diagnosis. One conversation we had involved Neil telling me that I would be going back to college at the start of the next semester. I told him that my journey with college was over. Things were different; it was in his brain. We would probably have to sell the business, as well. Who was going to drive the truck now?

We drove past a middle-aged man sitting in a red convertible at a set of traffic lights. Neil looked at him and said, 'When you have your health, you have everything'. I pondered on what he said, but made no comment. I thought of that statement years later and wished that I had said, 'No, with *God* you have everything'. Perhaps the fear and inner panic that I was feeling at the time prevented me from seeing that clearly.

Eventually, we drove into our suburb. It was around eight o'clock in the evening on Sunday, 28 December 2008. We stopped at the local service station to buy a loaf of bread and a bottle of milk that Neil went in and bought. We then drove the five minutes down the road to our house. We got out of the car and walked towards the house. I was looking forward to having a quiet evening with Neil at home without the girls. As we walked into our undercover area at the front of the house, we saw that a Christmas hamper had been left for us. We smiled and had a quick chat about what a blessing it was and then headed to the front door. I unlocked the door, and Neil asked me if I had passed wind. I giggled as we walked through the door while Neil laughed and told me that I should go back outside. It was the last thing that he ever said to me.

Chapter Eleven

THE STORM CLOSES IN

For You have been a strength to the poor, a strength to the needy in his distress, a refuge from the storm

Isaiah 25:4 (NKJV)

....●

Once we got inside our house, I walked past the telephone and noticed that there was no power to the phone. The next thing I noticed was that the ceiling in the lounge room had collapsed in the far corner of the room. We had experienced a lot of rain in November and December, and because the ceiling was poorly constructed, it had started to come down. This was no surprise; I had actually told Neil that it would likely fall down while we were away over Christmas. So, as I stood behind Neil with his back to me, I said, 'Look Neil, the ceiling has fallen in.' He didn't say anything, but I heard a sudden intake of breath, which I thought nothing of at the time. Perplexed as to why he did not answer me, I moved around to face him. I said again, 'Look Neil, the ceiling has fallen down!' He didn't respond. I studied his eyes and knew instantly that something was very wrong. His pupils were dilated and he stared straight ahead without response. Then he started drooling from the side of his mouth and began stumbling around the room. I quickly grabbed him and sat him on the lounge. I started yelling at him, 'Neil, can you hear me?', but he did not respond. I said to him, 'Neil, are you fooling with me? Stop it! This is not funny!' He was always stirring people up and tricking them, so I thought that was his game. I gently slapped him on his face, but still there was nothing, no response. A rush of panic struck me like a wave, and I realised that we were in serious trouble.

I then remembered, as I knelt in front of Neil, that the phone was out and that both of our mobile phones had flat batteries. I began to panic more and took in deep breaths in an attempt to calm myself. What was I going to do now? I thought about our next-door neighbours who had kindly been feeding our girls' two cats while we were away. I told Neil to stay seated and ran next door. I knocked on the neighbour's front door but got no reply. I raced back to the house; however, within the few minutes that I had been gone, Neil had somehow gotten himself down the front steps of the house and was now stumbling around outside on our driveway, tripping over his leather slides. I quickly grabbed him and, while he leant on me, I directed him back into the house and sat him back on the lounge. At that moment, I heard voices coming from our backyard. It seemed that the neighbours were entertaining guests in their backyard, which never happened. So, I took the risk and, again, left Neil sitting on the lounge. I ran into the backyard and over to the side fence. I yelled out to my neighbours, telling them to call an ambulance. I yelled out our street number and told them to tell the ambulance service that it was an emergency. I knew enough about the medical system to know that if they told the ambulance service that it was an emergency and gave no further details, the case instantly became a Code One and they had to race to the location immediately. I went back inside, and thankfully, Neil was still on the lounge, but he was getting very agitated, shifting in his seat and making grunting sounds. My neighbours and some of their family came over and asked if I needed assistance and asked what had happened. I was in shock and barely able to speak. I don't really know what I said to them, and then they left.

Within minutes, I heard the siren and it got louder and louder as the ambulance screamed towards us. I began to feel bad because I was not sure if calling the ambulance was warranted and I did not want to get into trouble. Two ambulances pulled up out the front, and I am sure that, had I looked, all of our neighbours would have been at their front windows, peering through the curtains. Suddenly, four paramedics ran into the lounge room carrying bags and machines. Neil's illness was recorded in the medical system, so the paramedics already knew about his battle with cancer, which was obvious by the way they spoke to me. Almost as soon as they entered the room, Neil deteriorated further. He began vomiting and was losing consciousness. The paramedics went to work, giving him oxygen, yelling at him to stay with them, and hooking him up to monitors. Whilst this was going on, I wandered around in circles in the lounge room, my hands on my head, wondering what on earth had just happened and thinking how relieved I was that the girls had not come home with us and were spared from witnessing this scene. The paramedics told me to get together some belongings to take to the hospital for the both of us, as well as Neil's medication. I only had time to grab what was necessary, including a jacket for me; I had spent enough time in hospitals to know how cold the air-conditioning was. Within minutes, Neil was wheeled out on a gurney and put into the back of the ambulance. I was asked to get into the front of the same ambulance to sit next to the driver. As we drove off, I looked at our car, the boat trailer still attached, which we had just gotten out of minutes before. In it sat the bottle of milk and the loaf of bread, as well as all our Christmas presents.

I vividly remember being in the front of the ambulance as it drove down roads that were very familiar to me. They were taking Neil to the Mater Adult Hospital where he'd had his chemotherapy treatment. I recall looking around at what was happening in the back of the ambulance. Neil was strapped down to the gurney and was very agitated, moaning and groaning and fighting the restraints. Then the paramedics yelled at him to stay with them when he started losing consciousness, telling him it would be okay. They started getting the pads ready to resuscitate him with the defibrillator; they did not think he would make it to the hospital. I turned back around to stare at the parked cars that we passed. I was very overwhelmed and suffering from severe shock. The driver must have noticed this because he tried to keep me engaged in conversation—not an easy task. We made it to the hospital, and Neil was quickly unloaded and raced into the Emergency Department. I recall paramedics saying something to the nurses and motioning towards me; the conversation possibly had something to do with me suffering from shock.

That evening was one of the darkest of my life as I felt my whole world coming down around my ears. That night, as Neil was treated in the Emergency Department, I had more than one doctor come to tell me that it was very unlikely that Neil would make it through the night. Eventually, I was allowed to sit with him. I held his hand, and when he lifted my hand to his mouth and bit my finger, I knew then how dire the situation really was. The independent, self-sufficient man that I had been married to for more than thirteen and a half years had lost all his faculties, did not know who I was, and was vomiting as well as urinating in the bed.

I got myself together enough to ask to use a phone to call the family and a few close friends to tell them what had happened. All of our friends thought we were still in Taree enjoying the Christmas holidays. They did not know about the cancer going to Neil's brain, and our families were at home, blissfully unaware of what was happening to their son, brother, uncle, son-in-law, brother-in-law, and father. The first call I made was to Neil's parents' house. By this time, it was around eleven at night, and my call woke up his mum. I explained to her through tears that something dreadful had happened to Neil and that he was in hospital in the Emergency Department. She told me it would be okay, and, I, barely holding it together, told her that it was really, really bad. She said that they would all drive up immediately. I told her that I did not want the girls to see their dad like this, but she said they needed to come so they could say goodbye. Things were bad, really bad, but I still had not lost hope and had no intention of saying goodbye, so I was not prepared for her to say that. After the call ended, I rang some of our closest friends and the pastors of our church.

Within a short time, all of those people came to the Emergency Department to offer their support and to pray. When I saw my friend Ronda walk through the sliding glass doors, I walked over to her in a flood of tears, trying my hardest to cover my face because there was some guy, a stranger, sitting in the room. I was sure that, without knowing the details, he knew I had experienced a huge tragedy. I hugged Ronda and told her through tears that I was not very happy; it was not supposed to happen this way.

Within a few hours, Neil was admitted onto a ward, and when my friends left around two o'clock in the morning, I went to sleep on a very uncomfortable chair, one of many that I would sleep on in the coming months. Later that morning, our girls and all of the Tyrie family arrived after their long drive interstate. I remained strong and 'together' while I hugged my girls and the rest of the family. They went to Neil's bedside to see him and assess the situation. Later that day, Dr Shannon came to see her 'exasperating' patient, telling me that tests showed that Neil had suffered a massive stroke and it did not look good. He had lost the use of his right arm and hand, could not walk or talk, and the right side of his face had dropped.

What transpired became a few weeks of torture. I stayed with Neil while the family cared for the girls. I needed permission to stay on ward because I was not a patient. I was adamant that I was not leaving Neil there one night without me. He was completely without his faculties, and I was worried about him falling out of the bed. I slept next to him in a recliner chair positioned as close as possible to Neil's bed so I could rest my hand on him in the hope that I would wake up if he tried to get up. In fact, one time, he got very agitated and tried to get out of bed. He got halfway before he started to fall. I raced over and held up my six-foot-four husband's upper body so that he did not hit the ground on his head, all whilst he groaned at me. I could not reach the patient buzzer, so I stood there struggling for a minute until I saw a nurse way down the corridor. I yelled out to her, but she did not hear me. Then, finally she looked up and saw me. All I could do was mouth the word 'Help.' She went into a panic and grabbed a male nurse who ran into the room, jumped over the bed, and helped me get Neil up into the bed.

At first, Neil could not eat or drink, and he was reduced to wearing nappies, otherwise, he would dirty the bed. Further, he could not communicate with me at all. He was diagnosed with a condition called Aphasia, which is a language disorder that results from strokes and brain tumours where a certain part of the brain is damaged. Even though aphasiac patients may be able to comprehend the world around them, they have no way of communicating. Dr Shannon came and explained the new complexities in Neil's journey with cancer: because he had cancer, they could not treat the stroke, and because he had a stroke, they could not treat the cancer. In other words, they were just going to keep him comfortable until he died.

Despite this news, I continued to believe that my God would save us and deliver us out of this situation. I prayed without ceasing, listened to worship music, and began to write in a journal to record what was happening and to encourage myself with what God was showing me in the midst of the storm. On New Year's Eve, I walked down the ward's corridor to the end of the building and watched, through the window, the fireworks display that lit up the sky over the Brisbane River. I did not feel like celebrating. I had no idea what the new year, 2009, would bring, and in that moment, I didn't want to know.

Neil did start to respond to us as the weeks went on. The doctors came to ascertain his level of understanding by asking him to lift his foot or something similar to that, but he did not seem to comprehend. Yet, he recognised his friends when they visited, which included the Barnes and Pattisons from Narrabri, and his buddy, Parrish from Wellington. Neil's ability to understand his surroundings and his situation became most obvious when his brother, Wayne, visited the hospital one day. At this particular stage, Neil was able to walk around a little with support and supervision. Neil, Wayne, and I were walking down the ward's corridor, dragging along the IV machine that Neil was hooked up to. It was his first trip out of his hospital room. It is a moment I will always treasure as he walked up to the elevator doors with the intention of leaving the hospital. I gently told him that he could not leave, to which he rolled his eyes and gave me a look that only a husband of thirteen years could give to his wife, obviously thinking, 'Come on, woman, give me a break!' He was led back to his room, and later, Wayne said that the look on Neil's face was priceless.

The other moment that I will always treasure occurred on my birthday. I woke up in the hospital on January 20 knowing it was my birthday and thinking I was going to make the best of it. I was turning thirty-four years old. After Neil was settled and ready for the day, I said, 'Neil, it's my birthday today.' He looked at me and lifted his hand and caressed the side of my face. It was the only time after his stroke that he showed me any kind of affection. It was the best birthday present that he ever gave me.

Chapter Twelve

THE STORM BUILDS

For I am persuaded that neither death nor life, nor angels nor principalities nor powers, nor things present nor things to come, nor height nor depth, nor any other created thing, shall be able to separate us from the love of God which is in Christ Jesus our Lord

Romans 8:38-39 (NKJV)

....•

T he storm continued to rage and intensify as Neil was moved to a palliative care ward at a different location the day after my birthday. Earlier, in mid-January, the doctor had told me that there was nothing that they could do for Neil, and he would need to go to a palliative care facility until his inevitable death. This caused me great distress because I was happy with where he was, but mostly, it was because I had not given up on him being completely healed. To see that Neil's medical team had given up on him unsettled me greatly. After some research, I found a facility that was closer to home than the hospital and I decided, begrudgingly, that Neil would go there; however, I was adamant that he would be walking out of that facility. He would not be dying there, or anywhere else, for that matter. After Neil was put into an ambulance and transferred to the new care facility, another unexpected battle began.

Because the new destination was a palliative care ward, the atmosphere was noticeably different from the start. In fact, a new wave of shock and reality came over me. Death was in the air; it was tangible. All the patients on the ward were terminal, and none of the nurses or doctors were concerned with restoring a patient's health; they were just going through the motions, keeping the patients comfortable until they died, which was expected, almost like a set goal. Not only did this bring a new battle for me in staying in faith and believing for Neil's healing, it also meant that strict hygiene policies observed in other hospitals were flung out the window. There was no real need to worry about infection and the like; in fact, it would probably help speed up the process. I struggled so much with this. Taking Neil to use the toilet that he shared with a female patient in the room next door was excruciating, to say the least. I even considered going home to get some cleaning products to clean the toilet myself. One day, I asked the cleaner nicely to please sweep the floor because Neil would drag dirt into the bed with his socks after walking on the floor. I carefully articulated that the floor had not been cleaned for days, to which she replied sternly that that was impossible. She then begrudgingly cleaned the floor, and I thought to myself that I would not ask the cleaner to clean again. I had not left Neil's side, and after seeing the same dirt in the same place for days, I knew that no one had been in to clean. However, I did tell the nurses when the toilet got so bad that I did not want to take Neil in there anymore.

My experience of that place was hellish. On one of the first days there, I was feeling very down because I had agreed to bring Neil to this horrible place. The atmosphere drained the life out of me, and I was struggling. It was a rainy day, which I was happy for because the smell of rain was my favourite scent, so to try to encourage myself, I slightly opened some slats of the louvred window so I could hear and smell the rain. Within minutes, this sergeant-major nurse came in and yelled at me and told me to shut the window, saying the hospital was air-conditioned. A day later, she was back, yelling at me because I was charging my phone and iPod in the power point. I did not know at the time that the devices had to be checked by a safety technician. It was a very difficult time all round.

Despite being in such a grim and gloomy place, some of the staff members were encouraging and they tried hard to make Neil's stay there as comfortable as possible. There was also the odd moment of light and joy. One day, when Wayne was visiting, Neil was eating his breakfast, which he was, by this stage, able to do on his own using one hand. Neil was supposed to take a particular steroid once a day to help keep the swelling down in his brain. He had been prescribed them when in the hospital in Taree. He had to take a laxative as well. Neil disliked taking medication, so it was important to make sure he did. I had many arguments with him when trying to get him to take them. On this one particular day, I asked him if he had taken his tablets, to which he nodded 'yes', but the cheeky look on his face told me otherwise. So, Wayne and I asked him where the tablets were, and he instinctively put his hand near the sheets on his bed. We lifted the sheets, and there they were, the two tablets. The cheeky look on his face told us that he knew the game was up and he had been found out.

The one huge blessing that was afforded us in that facility was that they offered a social worker and a justice of the peace service. A doctor went out of his way to assist me in selling the business. We had not organised a will or power of attorney, which we should have done considering our predicament, so I did not have the power to sell the business as it was in Neil's name, as were most things, including the vehicles and the boat. The kindly doctor organised a cognitive assessment to see if Neil could understand enough to sign power of attorney over to me. He thought that Neil did understand, so he organised for a Justice of the Peace to bring in the relevant papers. To my absolute amazement, not only did Neil understand, but to make sure we were fully aware of this, he wrote his signature legibly, using his left hand. A simple scribble would have sufficed. I felt very confident that it was Neil's desire to sell the business; we had discussed it at length before the stroke. Having power of attorney was a huge blessing to me because Wayne and Neil's friends could not work the business indefinitely. I also felt that it was a huge blessing to Neil to know that the girls and I would have some money, and that I would not be burdened with trying to run the business on my own. The business was eventually sold to a family friend. He was one of the friends who worked the business for us when Neil first had the stroke and was also the friend staying with us when Neil was first diagnosed. I found out later that Neil had actually discussed selling the business to this friend a year or so before, but he had not told me.

Despite the negative atmosphere in the palliative care facility, Neil continued to improve, so much so that one day the doctor said to Neil's dad, Garry, that he had seen Neil walk to the showers and had not realised it was him. He told Garry that he could not account for why Neil was doing so well. I was not surprised. I knew that God's hand was on us, even in such a dire situation. To survive my time there, I waited until Neil was settled in the evenings, then I would take my iPod and go for a walk along the water constantly praying and worshipping God, choosing to put my faith and hope in a God who had never let me down.

A few weeks into our time there, the girls resumed school for the start of the new school year. I got everything ready from the hospital, even using the dinner tray to wrap the girls' books with contact. I had prayed fervently over the weeks that Neil would receive instant healing so that he could be at the school with Callie on her first day. Unfortunately, he remained at the hospital while the rest of the family joined her. It was a very emotional day for me; Callie should have had her dad there on such a special day, and Neil should have been able to celebrate with me our last child heading off to school. That afternoon, Neil smiled as his three girls came through the door of his hospital room in their new school uniforms, all three of them. Neil's affection for his girls throughout his time in hospital also spoke volumes about his ability to understand and remember the important things.

The girls coped as well as they could with Neil's illness and the fallout of the stroke. However, Callie had to adjust to seeing her dad looking so different, with half of his face drooping and him motioning strangely because he could not communicate. It scared her. Emmy and Maya also had to adjust to their dad being this way, instead of the witty, teasing, jovial man he used to be. I missed that man so much it hurt, but I was far from thinking that he was gone forever.

As a result of school resuming, I changed my routine. I slept in the hospital on an uncomfortable chair beside Neil's bed every night while Neil's parents stayed with the girls at the house. Then, after waking up early and giving instructions to the nurses on duty, I drove home and got the girls ready for school. I dropped the girls at school, and then raced back to the hospital to give Neil a shower; I wanted him to keep his dignity, so I would not allow anyone else to shower him. As much as possible, I tried to do for Neil what I would want done for me in a similar situation, and because I loved him, there was nothing that I would not do for him.

Except for going out on a day trip to a park only minutes away, beside Moreton Bay, to celebrate Neil's mum's sixtieth birthday on Australia Day 2009, Neil did not leave the hospital until the day he walked out himself. When I had made the decision for Neil to go to that facility, I had known that he would walk out of there; my faith demanded it. In fact, I took his slippers there with us so that he could walk out in them. And on 4 February 2009, he did just that.

He went home just in time for his forty-second birthday which was on 8 February. Neil was so excited to be going home. When he did get home, he did a slow lap around the house and yard to see his place. We set up an electric lift recliner chair, borrowed from a family friend, that helped to raise him up when he wanted to stand up, and I continued his care at home. He wore nappies for a time but then did not need them. I showered him daily, dressed him, fed him, and shaved him, which was a new experience for me, and generally made him as comfortable as possible. Except for a few rushed trips in the middle of the night to the hospital in an ambulance because of infection, pneumonia, and septicaemia, he stayed home with his family. Neil's mum, Shirley, stayed to help look after her son and his dad travelled back and forth from Taree, depending on work commitments.

It is hard to put into words how difficult this time was in my life, except to say it was very dark. I was in a continual battle to keep Neil with me while keeping my faith strong, despite most people around me being negative. Even Christians around me had resigned themselves to the 'inevitable'. I understood where they were coming from. I have wondered many times if I was in denial throughout the battle because I could not face the truth. However, I do not think that was the case at all. I had just seen too many instances of God's mighty hand moving in my life to not have faith. It was that simple. I was going to go out believing, trusting my Heavenly Daddy til the very end.

When Neil had just finished his chemotherapy, he had read a book on healing, and one statement in the book had resonated with us both. The author stated that with regards to receiving healing, one should live out of faith, believing for the healing, and in the event that it did not come, and this life ended, one would have still held fast to the confession of one's hope in God without wavering (Hebrews 10:23), and this was what Neil and I tried to do. Even though I had no idea what was going through Neil's mind and spirit, I was certainly going to keep up my end of the promise, regardless of the circumstances, regardless of what I saw or heard. My God 'who promised *is* faithful' (Hebrews 10:23, NKJV), and that was all I needed to know. Scripture says that 'Jesus Christ *is* the same yesterday, today, and forever' (Hebrews 13:8, NKJV), and the circumstances around Neil's illness did not change that, not for one single minute. Despite my intention to remain in faith, I suffered. It would be a very cold-hearted person, indeed, who didn't suffer in watching a loved one struggle so.

Even though Neil came home from the palliative care facility having improved, after a month or so at home, his health deteriorated dramatically. I began to get very anxious but still focused on what the Bible said and what I knew of my loving Father. I spent many a time in the shower crying with my forehead rested against the tiles, the water running down my back. The rest of the family had no idea how I struggled. I came out of the shower looking calm and together, but it was not long before I realised that my shower moments were, in fact, anxiety attacks. The weight of the situation was getting the better of me. As the weeks went on, I realised that the college semester was about to start. My heart broke at the realisation that I would not be going back. On the morning of the first lesson, at the exact time of the lesson, I was showering Neil. I made an excuse as to why I needed to leave the ensuite and, losing composure at the realisation of another loss, I cried in the bedroom, inconsolable. Of course, I would have rather been with Neil, but it was a harsh blow to me. It felt like the end of my dream. Up until that moment, I had not realised how important my degree was to me.

The situation only got worse; Neil became very frail and unwell. One morning, he was lying on our bed, and as I passed him, I lovingly ran my hand down his thigh as he slept. To my shock and alarm, there was practically no flesh on his bones; the change had crept up on me. A visit from a family friend further clarified the situation to me. Having visited Neil in the bedroom, he came out and told me that Neil looked very unwell. This man's father and mother had died of cancer and he recognised the signs. I told him that I was certain that God was going to heal him despite this, and his response to me was, 'I hope you have a plan B.' No, I didn't. I was going to continue to believe, and when all else failed, I was going to continue to believe.

Chapter Thirteen

THE ROUND IS LOST

But you are those who have continued with Me in My trials.
And I bestow upon you a kingdom, just as My
Father bestowed one upon Me, that you may eat
and drink at My table in My kingdom

Luke 22:28-30 (NKJV)

··•

O ne night that I will never forget was the night of 4 April 2009. I had gotten Neil ready for bed and asked him if he would like me to read the Bible to him. He communicated 'yes' with a nod, so I sat on the floor next to the bed and opened the Bible that Neil had given to me as a gift. I began to read from the book of Psalms all the scriptures that I was resting my hope on, all the promises. I was exhausted by this stage in the battle; my resilience was at an end. I was tired. As I tried to read to Neil, the words came out in sobs. The words I was reading did not ring true for me anymore; my circumstances confirmed this. I was extremely emotional. Numerous times since, I've analysed Neil's response to my emotional breakdown as I tried to work out what he might have been thinking that night. As I cried and sobbed, wiping away tears that would not stop, he just lay there looking at me with no emotion. Did he wonder if I had given up? Did he think that I knew death was imminent? I don't know. I eventually apologised to him, saying that I was just tired. I held his hand and prayed with him for the umpteenth time, asking God to deliver us out of the nightmare we were in, then I left so he could sleep. Later, many times, I would reflect on that time we spent together, thankful that Neil had seen that I was not coping like I always did, that my heart was torn. I was not just a nurse tending to a patient with clinical detachment, but rather, I was a wife who could no longer bear the sight of her husband suffering, having not received the deliverance that we were certain would come. I was becoming desperate and overwhelmed.

Two days later, on the ominous date of 6 April 2009, it promised to be a busy day. We were expecting visitors from the church, beloved friends, some who had known Neil most of his life; one was his youth pastor from more than twenty years earlier. However, on this day, for the first time since he had come home from hospital, Neil could not even get out of his chair for a shower. I washed him with a face washer while he sat in the chair, and then I tried to give him breakfast. He did not want it, another first. Our visitors came and went, with one farewelling Neil with the words, 'The next time I see you, you will greet me at the gate'. Little did we know at the time the double meaning behind those words.

Later that day, Neil was getting very uncomfortable, and I was very concerned. The morphine I was giving him as a pain relief was doing very little. I called the GP who had offered to assist me after Neil came home, and he said he would make a house call. At around one o'clock in the afternoon, he came. I had asked him to bring a machine to do an oxygen saturation test. The doctor did not think it necessary, but obliged. To the doctor's surprise, Neil's oxygen levels were very low. He was also cold and clammy. The doctor wrote me a new script for stronger morphine. Throughout the journey, I had been adamant that Neil would remain conscious and coherent, only giving enough morphine to reduce the pain so he was comfortable not catatonic. On this trip, the doctor told me that that was not really an option anymore, much to my distress. As the doctor left, I followed him out the door. At the gate to our home, I was about to ask the doctor how much time he thought Neil had left, but I thought better of it. I had never really been interested in the negative reports from the doctors, and I had no intention of starting now. Many times later, I wished that I had.

After the doctor left that day, Neil's mum went to pick up the girls from school. She was then going to take them to my friend Sally's house for a play and a swim. This was the first afternoon that the girls had not come straight home from school, and I should have known then that something was up. I left the house at the same time to get the stronger drugs for Neil, leaving Neil sitting in his chair watching TV with his dad. I told his dad that Neil should be fine and I would not be long. I went to get the medication, and after organising a few things whilst out, I headed home. As soon as I walked in the front door, I knew something was wrong. Neil was in the bedroom, and from the moment I entered the house I could hear his laboured breathing from down the hallway, a sound I had not heard before. I had a quick talk with his dad to find out what had happened, and then I went in to comfort Neil. He was distressed, sweating profusely, and was very agitated because he was having trouble breathing. I got a towel to pat his forehead and went and got him some painkillers, giving him a kiss on the cheek as I left. I hauled him into a sitting position and got him to take the painkillers. I told him to try to calm down and that the painkillers would take effect soon. I thought he was having a pain attack of some sort. Because of his distress, I asked him if he wanted me to call an ambulance. I was surprised when he communicated 'yes' with a nod because he hated going to the hospital. I went out and told his dad with a surprised and alarmed tone in my voice that Neil motioned that he wanted to go to hospital. His dad was very quiet; I think he knew what I did not.

I called the ambulance and told them it was not an emergency but not to be too long. As I started to get together his medication for another trip to the hospital, I heard Neil's dad call my name with a particular urgency that told me something bad had happened. I ran down the hallway to the bedroom and walked up beside Neil who was still lying on the bed. He looked like he was having a seizure or a fit of some kind. It was not uncommon for stroke patients to experience seizures, so I thought that that was what we were dealing with in that moment. My first thought was, 'Okay, it looks like we are about to face another stint in the hospital.' Then, I said to Neil's dad, in range of Neil's hearing, 'That doesn't look good. Wait here with him. I'm calling the ambulance back.' I raced down the hallway, picked up the phone, and was greatly annoyed when it would not work properly at first—reminding me of the similarly stressful situation when the stroke first occurred. As I tried to call the ambulance, Neil's dad called my name again, this time with an emotion-filled voice that told me things were way worse. With foreboding, I walked down the hallway trying to prepare myself for what I was about to see, but that was really not possible. I was greeted by the sight of Neil lying motionless on the bed, his eyes staring blankly, his laboured breathing stopped. In that moment, reality set in: he was gone . . . just like that. I looked up at Neil's dad, and the first words to come out of my mouth were, 'You have got to be kidding me!' And then I remembered a request that I had made to God when I noticed Neil was really starting to deteriorate. I had been vacuuming the floor while Neil rested on the bed. I was thinking about what would happen to Neil if things continued as they were. Would Neil end up on an oxygen machine while the girls and I watched him suffer and get worse and worse? In that moment, I prayed to God, 'Lord, if You are going to take him, please take him quickly. If You are going to heal him, please heal him quickly.' Both God and I knew that I did not have it in me to nurse Neil on his deathbed as he wasted away. I told God this. As Neil lay there motionless on the bed, I was reminded of what I had asked of God, and instantly I thought, 'He has taken him quickly.'

At that moment, I heard the ambulance pull up out the front. I ran out and yelled for them to come quickly and told them that he had stopped breathing. They ran in, put Neil on the floor, and began to do resuscitation on him, having cut down the middle of the new superman shirt that I had bought for him for Christmas. Neil's dad had left the room when the paramedics arrived to secure a dog we were dog-sitting at the time. As they were pounding on Neil's frail body, I got more and more upset and eventually, after many minutes, begged them to stop. They told me that I should leave the room, but having never left Neil's side throughout the whole journey, I was not about to leave him then. I stood next to the window, out of the way, looking at the scene like I was hovering above it. It was an extremely surreal moment. It was the perfect Autumnal day and the sun's rays beamed down on the tragic scene through the west-facing window. My head was swimming with thoughts, and I was in deep shock. After a while, the paramedics gave up and declared Neil dead at approximately twenty-five minutes past five in the afternoon. I walked out of the room while they arranged Neil's body on our bed, on my side.

Within minutes, Neil's mum came home; Garry had called her. She had left the girls with Sally, not telling them what had happened; that would be left to me. Neil's sister, Loren, also arrived shortly after while I was sitting on the lounge in so much shock that I felt practically nothing; I was completely numb.

The police came, as is the procedure. At the time, I was on the phone to my good friend, Ronda. My first words to her when she answered the phone with, 'Hey, Beautiful!' were, 'Ronda, he's gone.' She was shocked and devastated.

I had to decide whether or not the girls should view Neil's body; I did not want to distress them too much. We, as a family, agreed that the girls should decide, so Neil's mum went and collected the girls while I sat on the lounge and waited for their return, thinking, 'How on earth am I going to break the news to them?' I will never ever forget seeing the girls come bounding through the door with smiles on their faces, without a care in the world. The hardest thing I have ever had to do was tell my girls that the father they had kissed goodbye before they went to school that morning was gone. It took me a few minutes to get the words out. No one rescued me; it was my job. As soon as I told them, Emmy and Maya cried, and Callie, only five years old, gave a nervous laugh. However, it did not take long for reality to set in.

The girls decided that they would see their dad; they were hesitant, but I explained that it would be the last time they would see him, on earth, anyway. Silently, holding their hands, I walked them down the hallway to the bedroom and opened the door. I do not remember much except the four of us standing beside the bed while the girls cried and kissed their dad goodbye. I thought it would be too difficult for the girls to witness their dad being taken out of the house in a body bag, so Shirley and Loren took them over to Loren's house for dinner while Garry and I met with the funeral directors about preliminary details for the funeral. We needed to get things organised because it was Monday, four days before Good Friday, the day we remember our Saviour's death and resurrection; another school holiday.

Before the funeral directors arrived, I went down to the bedroom to say goodbye to my husband. I remember sitting on the side of the bed, crying, holding his hand in mine, observing how long his fingernails were from the cuticle to the end of his finger, a family trait. I looked at the scar on his wrist from where he had cut it open as a child. I looked over his face, noticing the distinguishing features that set him apart as being mine. I knew that it would be the last time that I would see him this way. It would be the last time I would hold his hand and stroke his hair. I was taking mental pictures to store in my mind, images that I could bring to mind long after he was gone. Eventually, I said my final goodbye and left the room.

I will never forget the way that Neil left his beloved home for the last time. He was placed into the white hearse and one of the funeral directors walked in front of the car as it slowly drove off, an act of respect for the owner of the home as he vacated it for the last time. As this took place, Garry and I stood arm in arm, watching with tears in our eyes. I said goodbye to my husband of nearly fourteen years whilst he said goodbye to his son of forty-two years. It is in such moments that we try to capture in our minds an image of the scene so that it will remain with us forever. It was the first time in the whole journey that Neil was on his own. I could not go with him this time. It devastated me. Later, I received a sympathy card from a pastor who Neil knew and ministered with in his time as a pastor. He had written, 'Neil may have lost the round, but he has won the battle.'

Chapter Fourteen

TANGIBLE DARKNESS

You, LORD, keep my lamp burning; my God turns my darkness into light

Psalm 18:28 (NIV)

....•

Once the police and funeral directors had gone, and all our family and friends, as well as praying church members, had been notified of Neil's death, I went to my room. I did not sleep much; I could not sleep. I stayed up till quite late, lying in bed, sobbing and sobbing. That night was the absolute darkest time of my life. Nothing has come close to the anguish I felt as I lay in that bed by myself for the first time, whilst my husband, whose side I had rarely left, lay on a cold, metal surface in a place that I did not know, by himself. Of course, I knew that he was no longer with his body, which was just an earthly suit, but that did little to comfort me that night. In fact, the only way I got to sleep that night, or any night for quite a few months, was by listening to worship music. I would listen to it until I passed out with exhaustion. I would wake up early in the morning with the music still playing in my ears, at which time I would pull out the ear plugs and go back to sleep. It took me a while, months in fact, to work out that I was suffering from posttraumatic stress disorder. The images of Neil dying played over and over in my head and the only way I could avoid it was by filling my head with other information, such as worship, until I passed out from exhaustion, ensuring I was not left alone with my thoughts where I would then dwell on it.

The pain that I experienced that first night was tangible. My heart hurt physically, so much so that I thought it was going to stop, and to be honest, I would not have cared if it did. As I lay awake that night, I pondered on what it would have been like for Neil to die. He struggled for breath, so I lay there, holding my breath for as long as I could so I could experience what it must have been like for him. The pain was so torturous that I could barely see myself being able to face it in the coming days, weeks, and months. I knew what it meant to be a 'tortured soul'. Each time I woke up that night, reality hit me hard like a hammer to my heart. I would reach across the bed and find that Neil was not there, where he had been just the previous night.

Words cannot really describe my despair. And to make matters much worse, I felt utterly forsaken by the only person who I had ever been able to truly trust, my Heavenly Father. What had happened? Where was He? However, despite my struggle, I kept my eyes fixed on God in the midst of the darkness, as if my life depended on the light from a distant lighthouse on a dark, foggy night. Yes, my faith was tested as it had never been before, but it was reasonably intact, battered and bruised, but the smallest glimmer of hope still shone through the darkness. The light was not constant; it flickered that first night. However, in the throes of despair, I knew that my God was there and He knew my pain.

The day after Neil's death, I woke up to see the floor covered in white, used tissues, so many that it looked like it had snowed while I slept. I managed to get out of bed; there were things to do, such as organising the funeral arrangements. The funeral was to be on Thursday, the day before Good Friday. Neil was to be cremated. I found a lovely spot in a little cemetery that was surrounded by green paddocks, just like his family home. I would place a memorial stone there for the girls and me to visit; his ashes would go down to the family farm. A lady from the council met Neil's parents and me at the cemetery plot and proudly exclaimed that kangaroos and wallabies grazed there each afternoon. I told her that if my husband were still alive, he would have shot them, being a country boy and all. It was a beautiful site, and I knew the girls would definitely appreciate the wildlife. It was a very difficult day for me and I just went through the motions. Later that day, I listened to all of Neil's favourite songs to decide which ones should be played at the funeral. Songs are a great trigger for bringing up memories, and each song represented a special time in our lives.

On the morning of the funeral, reality set in. It was quite late in the morning and I still could not get out of bed. Shirley came in to check on me and I told her that I was not sure I could face the funeral, being certain that I would not be able to keep my composure in front of everyone.

Eventually, I got up and got ready for the afternoon service. I was surrounded by family members from my side of the family as well as Neil's. His beloved grandmother, Ma, had travelled up from New South Wales at ninety-two years old. I was not prepared to see her, one of the most important people in Neil's life. When Neil had said goodbye to her on the day he had his stroke, he had been very quiet as we drove away from her house on the farm to travel back to Brisbane. I had sensed this and encouraged him that he would see her again. He was doubtful, and unfortunately, he was right.

I arrived at our church where the funeral was to be held. I held onto Garry's arm as we walked into the church. As I saw the hundreds of people looking at me with sympathy, I said to him, 'I can't do this.' He did not respond and continued leading me in as every eye in the place watched me. I sat down with the girls in the front row, in front of the casket, which I had to pay more for because Neil was so tall. I sought out my sister who was sitting in the front row further down, motioning to her to see if she was okay. I hadn't seen her since we left Taree before the stroke. My two best friends from college, as well as two of my lecturers, walked in and sat down. Not only was I supported by my college, but numerous teachers from the girls' school came, along with the principal. Some of Maya's medical and speech support staff were there also, and of course, all of Neil's many friends came from far and wide. I noticed, as I waited for the service to start, how beautiful the church looked. Vases of flowers and lit candles adorned the stage. It was weird and surreal to see my regular place of worship set up for my husband's funeral.

It was a lovely service, and we made time for people to come up and share their experiences of their friend, Neil. My girls went up and placed a rose on the casket, and their Uncle Wayne and Aunty Loren spoke on their behalf, telling the crowd what they loved best about their dad. Emmy, age eleven, said, 'I loved going camping, especially last year to Poona. Dad would play tricks on me just like he did on Aunty Loren. He would surprise me with karate chops, but I would always get him back by tickling his feet. I love him and will miss him very much.' Maya, age nine, said, 'I love my daddy. He was the best. When we went fishing, we caught a jellyfish. He would jump on the trampoline with us. Sometimes, Dad let me have KFC. We would have fun and go to parks. Jesus loved my daddy just like me, and he always gave me a happy face, and I wish that Dad would come back.' Then Callie, age five, said, 'Daddy would always jump on the trampoline with me. He always prayed for me at bedtime. Daddy always did special stuff with me and bought me a bike, and he always gave me kisses and huggles. I love Daddy very much.'

The day before the funeral, I had written down my thoughts about what had happened in Neil's journey and death. I wanted people to know that I had not lost my faith despite the fact that Neil was not healed. Our beloved friend and mentor, Ps Jim Baker, our former pastor from Narrabri, conducted the service and read out my thoughts to our family and friends, saying:

'Today, we gather to celebrate Neil's life, and in doing so we celebrate that he now enjoys joy unimaginable in the arms of Jesus, his Lord and Saviour, to whom he has been devoted his whole life. However, my mind cannot comprehend how a man who had such a love for people, and influenced so many, could have his life taken from him at such a young age. His only desire was to preach and minister to the lost and broken-hearted, and he would have travelled the world proclaiming God's goodness to all. One may ask what purpose could there be in having three beautiful girls lose their father at such a tender age? How does one explain the loss of a man who lived with integrity, a man who made every person he knew feel like they were his best friend?

'I do not know, but what I do know without wavering is that God held Neil's life in His hand, and even though we have no answers, God does. I know for sure that Neil would not want the events of the past months and days to cause people to question their faith or cause them to turn their eyes and hearts from God. At the end of the day, Neil would say that our relationship with God is all that matters, the only thing that is eternal. Besides, he would want to see all his mates again someday.

'Even at this time of incredible loss, I choose not to question the God who has given me everything that I have. Despite everything, despite all that I have lost, Jesus is still the lover of my soul. He is my constant and the solid rock on which I stand. One scripture in the Bible that has always ministered to me is found in the book of Job, in chapter one, where Job discovers that he has lost most of his family and all that he owns, and responds by saying, 'I came naked from my mother's womb, and I will be naked when I leave. The LORD gave me what I had, and the LORD has taken it away. Praise the name of the LORD!' (Job 1:21, NLT) Job's response reminds us to focus on what is eternal. Neil knew where his treasures lay, not in earthly treasures that fade away but in the eternal promises of God. And at this time, I choose to do the same.'

I followed Neil's casket out with the girls as it was held by his dearest friends and his brother, and then I walked up towards the end of the driveway to form a guard of honour. Friends and family clapped as Neil passed by in the hearse. As the vehicle passed by me, a family friend hugged me, and I remember looking over her shoulder, taking a mental picture of the very last time I would see my husband on this earth.

To spare my girls further heartache, I decided that we would not attend the crematorium; they had been through enough. As much as it broke my heart to not go with Neil on his final journey, I could not put my girls through it. We stayed at the church for the wake, and I distracted myself by talking to long-lost friends so that I did not think of my husband being cremated at that very moment.

After the funeral, I drove home with Garry, and whilst sitting in my driveway, with rain pattering on the windscreen, Garry told me how proud he and Shirley were of me and the way that I had looked after their oldest son. I told him that I would have done anything for him, and with every fibre of my being, I believed that. Unfortunately, for all my trying, I could not keep him here.

What followed was the whole family making the best of Easter, me asking that Neil's chair at the dinner table be left empty, and me getting quite emotional when the one-week anniversary of his death came around and I wished that what I knew then, in that moment, I had known before he died. I had spent the whole week asking myself if I could have done anything different. Should I have called the ambulance earlier? Should I have insisted that the doctor admit Neil into hospital when he came that day? Did he have pneumonia? Did I pray hard enough? Did I have enough faith? I beat myself up terribly, not even allowing myself to eat at times. How dare I enjoy life when Neil could not? I even got very upset when the church aided us financially, even though I was so, so grateful. With the sale of the business, I was reasonably comfortable financially. Neil had worked hard all his life, but he had refused to even treat himself to a new boat motor or to a trip overseas to Israel, and there I was with this extra money. It just seemed really unfair. Within the week, I realised that I was suffering from survivor's guilt. Neil and I had gone through the battle together and we were both supposed to come out of it together; not just me.

At the end of that difficult week, the girls and I went on a trip for five days to a lovely cottage by a creek in Tamborine Mountain, paid for by my wonderful church family. It was a great time with the girls, but terribly sad also, of course. I could no longer watch the show that was playing on the TV when I had left Neil sitting in his chair that ominous day, and still, years later, I find it hard to do so. The girls and I enjoyed horse riding, and as I sat on the cottage's little balcony shedding buckets of tears, the sound of the nearby running creek and the beauty of the surrounding rainforest soothed my aching heart.

At the end of the week, as we drove back towards home, I sensed the tension building in the car. We were going back home and Neil was not going to be there. It would be the start of a new and uncertain life for all of us. Through tears, I told the girls that I knew how difficult it would be for them to go home and face our new reality, and I encouraged them by saying that if it was within my power to do so, I promised to give them the best life that I could. I have been attempting to do so ever since. They have not suffered or missed out on doing anything because they were without their father. Of course, that does not include the suffering they experience because they are forced to grow up without him; they miss him terribly. They were Daddy's girls.

Chapter Fifteen

JOURNALING A NIGHTMARE

*The minute I said, "I'm slipping, I'm falling,"
your love, God, took hold and held me fast*

Psalm 94:18 (The Message Bible)

··•

8 January 2009

Here I am, sitting in the hospital, starting a journal that describes the most difficult time of my life. The last week since my husband, Neil, suffered a stroke has been both difficult to the point of being oppressing, and a time of blessing as I draw closer to God with every prayer I pray. Neil has made great progress and that has been such a blessing to me and all of his family and friends.

We are all taking things a day at a time, holding on to our faith, overlooking all the negative reports from doctors.

If there is something I know how to do, it is to trust God during dark times. My childhood was one continual time of darkness, and then many years later, our daughter, Maya, was diagnosed with cancer, aged 11 months. Through both of these times of testing, I saw the goodness and sovereignty of God. And as a result, I can sit here today and know that I am not alone.

'My God who promised is faithful' (Hebrews 10:23, NKJV),

and everything I have, I received from Him. He strengthens me and provides me with all that I need. Daily, I spend time with God in this hospital room, asking Him to heal Neil by His miraculous power. I don't believe that it is God's will for Neil to go home to Him yet. He has an amazing call of God on his life, and I believe that this time of testing will be used for good; giving Neil a mighty testimony that will see many set free and brought into God's kingdom.

Nothing in life is certain except God's love for us and the plans He has purposed before we were even born. Looking back over my life, I can see where God has kept me and protected me, and during this time, where the burden attempts to suffocate me and make me anxious and doubtful, I know that God is with me, and I can put all of my trust in Him.

Because of the severity of Neil's stroke, I am forced to take on the running of our business and all financial responsibilities, not to mention taking on the care and nurturing of our three daughters who want to know when Dad is going to get better and come home. Praise God, I have a lot of support from Neil's family, our many friends, and members of the church we call 'home'.

I am forced to sell the business that Neil and I have built up over the last seven or so years. A friend is interested in taking it on, and I am seeking God's guidance and wisdom to make the right decisions without Neil's direction. However, I believe that as I put my trust in God, He will make the way smooth and attend to all the issues I am dealing with. He is not only faithful to attend to the big issues, but He cares enough to deal with the small things as well.

9 January 2009

Neil is a little drowsy today and not as alert as he has been. It is concerning, but again, I believe God is in control and working on our behalf. The doctors have come and spoken to me about options available to us, such as Neil coming home, or going to a hospice or nursing home. My heart sinks when considering the latter options, but one option the doctors have not brokered is Neil being healed and walking out in complete health. I choose to believe that God will heal Neil. I refuse to give up despite the bad reports and what I can see in the natural. When reading a commentary in Neil's Bible, I read that we can trust God to be with us through any trial and because he has been faithful to us, we should remain faithful to Him. And if there is one thing I know, it is that God is faithful. The commentary is describing how God was faithful in delivering Daniel in the Bible from all the trials he faced. I am encouraged to know that the God of Daniel is also our God, able to deliver us from this trial and time of hardship. My trust is in the Lord and in Him only. This situation will work out for good and bring glory to God.

13 January 2009
Much has happened over the last few days. Last Saturday morning, Neil had a turn in the shower and exhibited symptoms like he did when he had his stroke. He has regressed a bit and isn't as responsive as he has been previously. I am still believing that God will miraculously heal Neil, despite this setback. He has also been quite unsettled and appears to be in pain. Several complications (such as rashes, infections and constipation) have added to his discomfort. I could lose hope just looking at him, but I know that my God is greater than the situation.

We have decided (the family and I) to move Neil to a hospice closer to home where they specialise with patients like Neil. It is a palliative care hospice, but I send him there with the belief that he will get better and be able to come home from there. I will go and have a look at the place today, and I am expecting to see God's provision, as He is in control of this whole situation. I trust God to open and close doors to fulfil His will and purpose.

Last night, I went out to dinner with all my best friends, as two of my oldest friends travelled up from down south to see Neil and me. I felt blessed to be amongst the women who have supported me and been so great, not just during this recent trial, but also during good times. Unfortunately, the movie we watched, *Marley and Me*, was about a beloved dog that died. Probably not the type of movie I should be watching. All of the girls were worried about how I was coping with it. I managed to sit through it without losing it. But only just!

It has been two and a half weeks since I have had a conversation with my husband and I miss him terribly. I miss the man I know and love. I have been encouraging him to stick with it because God is going to heal him. He seems to understand what I am saying. I constantly tell him that I love him and that we will get through this, that he will go on to speak of God's goodness and mighty power to deliver.

I have been reading the Psalms lately for encouragement and I am strengthened by Psalm 116. Particularly verses 7 and 8 which say, 'Let my soul be at rest again, for the LORD has been good to me. He has saved me from death, my eyes from tears, my feet from stumbling.' (NLT)

God is good to us. I choose to put my life in His hands.

The scripture that had recently brought great encouragement to Neil I found in Psalm 27 this morning, which brought a smile to my face. It is verse 13, which says, 'Yet I am confident I will see the LORD's goodness while I am here in the land of the living.' Verse 14 goes on to say, 'Wait patiently for the LORD. Be brave and courageous. Yes, wait patiently for the LORD.' (NLT)

I will wait patiently for the Lord. His timing is perfect.

'I have chosen to be faithful; I have determined to live by your regulations. I cling to your laws. LORD, don't let me be put to shame!' Psalm 119:30-31 (NLT)

18 January 2009
Well, God continues to be my strength during this time, and His goodness can be seen wherever I look. Neil has brightened up more every day and is doing very well. He is communicating to the best of his ability and is very alert, comprehending a lot of what is said. To look at him, one would not know that he is ill. God is good, and even though Neil hasn't regained the use of his arm and tongue, I know

that that will happen. Neil will be miraculously healed and restored to complete health. I have, in the past week, visited two hospices to see if they are suitable. I have now chosen which one Neil will go to. He will go as soon as a bed becomes available. It is a palliative care ward, but I believe that Neil will go there only to get better and return home.

The girls start school next week, and I don't know how I am going to cope with taking Callie to her first day without Neil. I have cried out to God with this burden and am expecting God's provision to be my strength. All I know at present is that I am never alone whilst I go through this, and God knows all of my needs.

We are continually supported by our church. Members bring meals to our home to help relieve the burden on Neil's parents as they look after our girls.

I am getting tired and a little emotional, but I refuse to give in to fear and anxiety. I choose to believe that my God is faithful and He will answer our prayers. I have followed God all of my life and this is where what I have believed all those years is put to the test. And I will come out of this test faithful to the God who has always been faithful to me. One of my favourite scriptures is in Job 23:10 which says, 'When He hath tried me, I shall come forth as gold.' (King James Version) And regardless of what happens, that is my greatest desire because God is the one constant in my life, and He has blessed me with everything I have.

I look forward to the day when the enemy loses and we are not put to shame, but all will look and see that God has moved His mighty hand to heal and restore Neil, where nothing is broken and nothing is missing. Thank you, Lord.

19 January 2009
Neil has had a good couple of days. He has started feeding himself, which I think is good for his own independence. With the girls going to school next week, Neil will need to be able to look after himself until I drop the kids to school.

Neil also had a wonderful day yesterday with the girls. They each took a turn to sit on Dad's lap and hold his hand. Occasionally, he would give each of them a kiss. It was good for both Neil and the girls, with Callie finally overcoming her shyness around Neil. She took it upon herself to entertain her dad by doing dances for him and singing him songs. You could not wipe the smile off Neil's face.

Every day is a day closer to Neil receiving his miracle. I claim it in Jesus' mighty name.

Psalm 3:1-5 says, 'O LORD, I have so many enemies; so many are against me. So many are saying, "God will never rescue him!" But you, O LORD, are a shield around me; you are my glory, the one who holds my head high. I cried out to the LORD, and he answered me from his holy mountain. I lay down and slept, yet I woke up in safety, for the LORD was watching over me.' (NLT)

Happy Birthday Monika!

'But let all who take refuge in you rejoice; let them sing joyful praises forever. Spread your protection over them, that all who love your name may be filled with joy. For you bless the godly, O LORD; you surround them with your shield of love.' Psalm 5:11-12 (NLT)

'You have given me greater joy than those who have abundant harvests of grain and new wine. In peace I will lie down and sleep, for you alone, O LORD, will keep me safe.' Psalm 4:7-8 (NLT)

20 January 2009
Well, it is my 34th birthday and we are still here at the Mater Hospital. Tomorrow, we move to the palliative care facility. All the family will be up later to celebrate with me. I told Neil that it was my birthday, and he lovingly put his hand up to caress my face. I know he understands. I will not get discouraged about being here on my birthday; I guess it is one I will not easily forget. I find that there are many opportunities for blessing during a time like this, and I am

expecting to have a great day. The girls rang this morning and sang 'Happy Birthday' to me, so it has started off well!

I got a bit of a revelation last night that this is not my burden to carry. God's Word explicitly states that we are to cast our cares upon Him and that He is well able to deal with all of our concerns, difficulties and trials. I know that God is in control, and I have no desire to take back the burden and carry it myself by worrying and being anxious. This is the beauty in being a child of the Most High God. He holds us in the palm of His hand and works on our behalf to restore and accomplish His will in our lives. I have said many times that if I thought that God wasn't with me as I went about my day, I would not get out of bed in the morning! This is never truer than now.

I feel that we have been robbed as a family and as children of God, but I know in my heart and my spirit that God will restore what has been lost and we will be able to experience a hundredfold blessing over our lives. It would not be God's will for us to remain beaten down for long, He will save the day!

Thank you, Lord, for letting me get this far in life. You have been my constant guide and strength, my protector.

'I love you, GOD—You make me strong.' Psalm 18:1 (MSG)

21 January 2009

I had a good day yesterday. Because Em was sick the two days previous, Shirley kept the girls home till the afternoon when Shirley, the girls, Loren, Wayne and Kath, their kids, and John came here to the hospital. We had a little party down in the TV room. I was worried the candles would set off the fire alarms and the whole hospital would need to be evacuated! I received some lovely gifts, and it was nice to celebrate with family and with Neil. I am just sitting here with Neil, waiting for the ambulance officers to come to take Neil to the other hospital. A new direction in the journey! I am sure there will be blessings to be experienced in the new place, although, I am anxious about the change. However, God goes before us and with us, so I am strengthened knowing that.

'Do not be afraid or discouraged. For the LORD your God is with you wherever you go.' Joshua 1:9 (NLT)

22 January 2009
Feeling a little down and emotional today after our big move. The staff are very friendly and helpful and their goal is to make our stay as comfortable as possible. They are also working hard to help me get power of attorney so that I can sell the business. God is good! I think I feel emotional because now that Neil is here, I need to take a step back and let others look after him so that I can be released to look after the girls when school starts next week. This, I am finding, is very difficult. I don't want him to think that I have abandoned him here. I hand it over to God who is so faithful. Thank you, Lord, that everything will be okay.

Shortly after Neil was first diagnosed with cancer in September 2007, God spoke to me at a church conference when I cried out to Him in desperation. He said clearly: 'This is bigger than both of you. It is for My glory. Everything will be okay. You just need to trust me' (Oct 2007).

I hold onto this as if it is the air I breathe. It has provided me with great comfort, and I have often reminded Neil of what God said to encourage him.

I will not doubt, but I will have faith.

Psalm 16:8 says, 'I know the LORD is always with me. I will not be shaken, for he is right beside me.' (NLT)

23 January 2009
Something wonderful happened yesterday. The social worker and doctors agreed that Neil had the cognitive ability to give me power of attorney. The JP came to have Neil sign the paperwork and a simple mark with a pen would have been enough, but, instead, Neil

signed his signature with his left hand, which was a wonderful way of showing that he did understand what he was doing. God is so good! The legalities of power of attorney and selling the business could have been very overwhelming for me, but I put my trust in God and gave Him my concerns to handle, and, being the faithful God that He is, He made it possible. He not only looks after the big things but also the small!

Even though some of the staff are lovely, I feel very unsettled here. It is my prayer that Neil won't need to be here long but will come home after receiving the healing entitled to him as a child of God.

I claim his healing, Lord. Please don't tarry! Let God's Word be true and every man a liar!

29 January 2009
The girls have started school and all went well, considering. I managed to maintain my composure without shedding a tear. We are still at the palliative care facility, and I have decided to sleep here and drive home to get the girls ready for school. I do not want to leave Neil here on his own for too long.

It has been a difficult week despite Neil doing well and improving more each day. I put that down to the atmosphere of this place; nobody here is expecting Neil to recover. They only wish to make him comfortable until his end comes. I feel depressed here, and my faith has wavered. But, I still hold on and continue to believe for Neil's healing and restoration.

Being Thursday, many people, including myself, are fasting and praying for Neil's healing today and will do so every Thursday until he receives it. I feel encouraged that there are many prayers going up for Neil today.

We have moved rooms. Neil is now in a single bed room on his own, which is great but there is no TV, which could be good. I think at a time like this, the more God one has, and the less world one has, the better. However, I don't want Neil here by himself without some form of stimulation. Neil has struggled in himself, too, since arriving here. He was quite emotional last night when someone prayed for him. I am going to saturate this room with music and Christian DVDs that will help keep his spirits up.

Every day, this gets harder and harder, but I will continue to believe in my God. I found a scripture that I loved as a teenager, Job 23:10. The whole passage is an encouragement to me:

'I go east, but he is not there. I go west, but I cannot find him. I do not see him in the north, for he is hidden. I look to the south, but he is concealed. But he knows where I am going. And when he tests me, I will come out as pure as gold. For I have stayed on God's paths; I have followed his ways and not turned aside. I have not departed from his commands, but have treasured his words more than daily food. But once he has made his decision, who can change his mind? Whatever he wants to do, he does. So he will do to me whatever he has planned. He controls my destiny.' Job 23:8-14 (NLT)

Even during this very difficult time, I know that God is in control and He will ultimately prevail over the enemy.

I thank you, Lord, that we are not alone; You are our strength, our refuge.

1 February 2009

'For verily I say unto you, That whosoever shall say unto this mountain, Be thou removed, and be thou cast into the sea; and shall not doubt in his heart, but shall believe that those things which he saith shall come to pass; he shall have whatsoever he saith.' Mark 11:23 (KJV)

The power of God's Word: 'My son, attend to my words; incline thine ear unto my sayings. Let them not depart from thine eyes; keep them in the midst of thine heart. For they are life unto those that find them, and health to all their flesh.' Proverbs 4:20- 22 (KJV)

12 February 2009

Much has happened recently; the best thing is that Neil has come home! He came home on the 4th of February, and I have been busy ever since! He did have to go back to hospital by ambulance at 4.30am the next day for an infection, but he came home again the same day. He is so happy to be home and is doing extremely well, but for a sore right leg that gets swollen when he walks on it too much.

It is so good to get Neil out of the palliative care facility where the talk and thoughts regarding Neil were so negative. The day before he left, his doctor there told Garry that he could not account for why Neil was doing so well, that there should be no reason for him to improve as he has! Praise God! I told Garry that he will be the first of many doctors to say that! I truly believe that!

Because we are home now, my days are kept busy looking after Neil and the house. Unfortunately, I haven't had time to spend with God as I would like. I am hoping to change that. The many visitors to the house also leave me with little time to spend with both Neil and God. I am absolutely exhausted and hope to be revived by spending time with God and reading His Word.

The business is still in the process of selling and should settle in the next coming days. Praise God! I will be relieved to be able to have more time with Neil and less time with paperwork.

Again, today is prayer and fasting day for Neil's healing. Lord, please hear and answer the prayers of Your people as they seek You today.

OUR GOD REIGNS

21 February 2009
I have been blessed to spend a bit of time with God over recent days and have gained revelations that have strengthened me. I listened to Dr James Dobson on the radio. He said that even when we think that God is late, He never is. His timing is always perfect. It certainly encouraged me.

We celebrated Maya's 9th birthday on Wednesday. We had a good day. Shirley and Loren shared in the celebrations. The highlight for her was getting her ears pierced!

On this journey, I have wondered if I have done everything possible on my part to help facilitate Neil's healing. I have been reading Che Ahn's book, *How to Pray for Healing*, and he states that 'relational faith' is so important. We are not to put our faith in healing, but in the God who heals because we know Him. I do put my faith and trust in God because I know He is faithful and He is good, and I believe it is His will to see Neil restored. Hebrews 10:23 says, 'Let us hold fast the confession of our hope without wavering, for He who promised is faithful.' (NKJV)

In his book, Che Ahn states, 'I don't understand the reasons behind God's choosing to heal at certain times and not others, but my posture and conviction is this: If I am sick, I am going to persevere and believe God for the healing until the healing comes, regardless of the timing. And I would much rather die having believed and not received than to go through life having thrown in the towel through unbelief and doubt.'

Amen, and amen!

5 March 2009

There is much to recount since I last wrote. Three days ago, we celebrated Emmy's 11th birthday. I went out of my way to make sure that she had the best possible day as she is the oldest and most perceptive and, therefore, understands clearly what is going on with Neil. I bought her some lovely gifts (charm bracelet, signet ring, necklace) and took her for a manicure! Her first! She had a great day.

On Monday morning when I noticed the time and realised that I would have been driving into college, I was very emotional and, for a time, inconsolable. My heart is broken as a result of having to set aside my dreams. However, I hand it over to God—my dreams, my desires, my pain and my disappointment—and I rely on Him for comfort. I know that His timing is perfect and that He knows the desires of my heart, and He will open doors as He sees fit.

Neil has been quite well and continues to be a testament to God's goodness and power. However, in the last few days, he has developed a bad cough and struggles at times to breathe as a result. I find myself getting anxious because my mind tells me that the cancer in the lung is the cause. However, I do not put my faith in what I see or hear but in God and His Word, and God's Word says that Neil is healed. Some days are extremely difficult for me, but I have decided that I will stand up and believe, despite the circumstances. I refuse to give up believing for Neil's healing.

I have been very tired lately, and as a result, I find my faith wavers a little. I am now trying to find time to rest and seek God for strength.

Neil had a day out last weekend at Paddy's house with John. He had a good day hanging out with the guys!

We went in to see Neil's oncologist, Dr Shannon, yesterday. She offered Neil radiation treatment because he was doing so well with the stroke side of things (Radiation was considered an option to give Neil more time). However, he declined the treatment. I wasn't surprised and neither was the doctor. Before his stroke, Neil had stated that he was not keen on getting any more treatment if the cancer came back. We discussed it at length. The toll the treatment took on his body was too much and if it was only going to extend his life for a short while, he didn't want to go through that struggle again. He wanted to leave it in God's hands, preferring that if he did get healed, God would get the glory.

I have a peace about it because my hope is in Christ. It was obvious that Neil still held to his previous convictions. He got very animated and emotional when he understood that he was going to see the doctor about possible radiation. I understood where his anxiety came from and assured him that I understood that he did not want further treatment. He settled down instantly, clearly relieved to know that I was not going to organise for him to have treatment, considering his inability to communicate effectively his wishes.

I am currently listening to a new CD. It's the soundtrack from the movie *Amazing Grace*, and the lyrics from one of the hymns say, 'I need thee every hour', referring to God. And I can certainly attest to that! Lord, You are my strength and refuge. Keep my family safe in the palm of Your hand.

'My flesh and my heart fail; But God is the strength of my heart and my portion forever.' Psalm 73:26 (NKJV)

'I WILL lift up my eyes to the hills—From whence comes my help? My help comes from the LORD, who made heaven and earth.' Psalm 121:1-2 (NKJV)

'I would have lost heart, unless I had believed That I would see the goodness of the LORD In the land of the living. Wait on the LORD; Be of good courage, And He shall strengthen your heart; Wait, I say, on the LORD!' Psalm 27:13-14 (NKJV)
(One of the scriptures that ministered to Neil).

19 March 2009

It has been a while since I have written because life has continued on at the same hectic pace. Having improved every day after coming out of hospital, Neil has gone backwards in the last week and a half. He was quite ill Wednesday week ago, so I took him to the GP and tests were done. On Thursday evening, the doctor rang and said Neil had septicaemia (bacteria in the blood). So, we had to go into hospital on Thursday night where Neil started a course of IV antibiotics. He came out of hospital on Monday just gone. He still has a nasty cough that developed about two weeks ago, which is concerning, and he appears to have significant pain in his chest area. Callie has had a bad cough and his latest cough and raspy throat could be attributed to that, perhaps. When he has a bad day or experiences a coughing fit, I start to get very anxious but choose to cast my concerns and cares at the feet of Jesus. I will not give up regardless of what I see or hear. I will not focus on the circumstances but on God's Word which states that Neil is healed and that God is a protector of His people. The scripture that continually comes to mind is, 'Let us hold fast the confession of our faith without wavering, for He who promised is faithful.' (Hebrews 10:23, NKJV) Amen, and amen.

Both Shirley and Garry are here helping at the moment, which is a great help to me in dealing with the day to day running of the house and looking after the girls.

Some days are better than others. Some days, when Neil is very unwell, I find it difficult to cope with the simplest things. My comfort eating has reached an all-time high and I am trying to rein myself in!

I have started another painting as a creative outlet and as an opportunity to sit quietly and reflect and listen to encouraging music.

Actress Natasha Richardson died today after falling over on a ski field and hitting her head. Within an hour of her fall, she was in a serious condition after laughing it off. It is terribly sad. Neil has had major trauma to his brain from the stroke and has battled brain tumours and swelling and continues to defy the doctors' predictions. This all goes to highlight how God has continually kept Neil in His hand and continues to do a mighty work.

Again, many are fasting and praying for Neil's healing today, including myself, and I know that every prayer makes a difference. Lord, please answer the prayers of Your people!

A verse that brings me great encouragement at the moment is Psalm 18:28, which says, 'You light a lamp for me. The LORD, my God, lights up my darkness.'(NLT)

Praise the Lord! He is good!

2 April 2009

We are still taking one day at a time, still standing on our faith. Neil has had some bad days lately where he is in a lot of pain and his breathing is laboured. However, I choose to continue to believe for his healing despite the circumstances. I admit that on days when Neil is very unwell, my heart sinks and I struggle to keep it together, but even during those times, I feel that I am far from alone; God is ever-present during this time. Praise God, that I can call on Him in such times. He is my strength.

This journey has endured for longer than I thought, and, therefore, I have needed a few personal adages that encourage me and keep me focused. They are:

God said it, I believe it, end of story!

I choose not to look at the circumstances, but I put my focus on God because His Word says that faith is the substance of things unseen, not seen. I don't care what I see or hear.

The circumstances *do not* change who God is.

Amen, and amen!

I have had some very busy weeks with many things needing my attention: cars breaking down, cochlears breaking down, Em needing a plate for her teeth, homework with the kids, exercising, painting (Although the last two are squeezed in on the rare occasion!).

Shirley is still here helping, which helps me a lot. Garry is coming back on Saturday and is staying till Easter in a week and a half. CHOCOLATE!!!

I went out for a lovely meal with my college friends Eileen and Vicki last night. It was great to catch up. I miss college a lot.

On a very sad note, Maurie Beard, whom I love dearly, died last Friday after suffering a heart attack due to his battle with cancer. It makes me so angry to see so many good Christians robbed of the life of blessing entitled to them as children of God. I feel so helpless, and I feel that my believing for Neil's healing is battered by such things. I wish I knew the keys to unlocking God's healing power to set people free of such infirmity. However, I feel like Moses, who said something like, 'Why me? Pick someone else. I am too inadequate.'

God just told me that even though I am inadequate, He is not.

. . . Just having a moment.

Lord, I will do whatever you ask.

8 April 2009

Well, despite all our prayers and faith, Neil passed away on Monday afternoon 6th April 2009 at around 5.25pm. I am heartbroken because I truly believed he would be healed. Not only have I just lost my husband, but I feel like I have lost everything I have ever believed in. If I can't believe that God heals as His Word declares, how can I believe anything that is written in His Word? However, I choose not to turn my back on God, I choose instead to say, 'The LORD gave, and the LORD has taken away; Blessed be the name of the LORD.' Job 1:21 (NKJV)

I am tormented with the thought that I could have done more, more praying, more fasting. But is it in works or is it in having the faith that moves mountains?

It is possible that Neil had an infection. He would have had a blood test on Tuesday morning. I will never forgive myself if that was the case and antibiotics would have eased his pain and he could still be here. I will never know for sure, but he didn't get a fever, which didn't really mean much in Neil's case as he has had infections without being febrile.

I keep going over the last few weeks in my head and wonder if I should have had him checked out sooner, as the GP came on Monday, only a few hours before he died. Later, the doctor said that he did not expect Neil to die that day.

I'd give anything to have him back with me, and I don't know how I am going to get through the coming months and years without him.

The funeral is tomorrow and I know that I will be barely able to function. I have gone through the motions of organising the funeral, the memorial plot, and the outfit I am wearing to the funeral, all the time disbelieving that he is actually gone. God was supposed to heal him; instead, he is lying on a cold slab in a foreign place awaiting cremation. If reality actually set in, I am sure I would collapse, especially after the trauma of the last eighteen months of enduring against all odds. What upsets me a lot is the knowledge that the doctors were right and can now ask, 'Where is your God?' It really is too much for me. Why? All Neil wanted to do was preach Christ to the world, and now so many people—medical staff, bag customers, and unsaved friends—will continue to disbelieve in a God who rescues and heals. I'd shout at the top of my lungs, break things, run away, hide, and give up, but nothing is going to relieve me of the pain I feel. The day after the funeral is Good Friday and then on Sunday, we celebrate Christ's resurrection. I would have encouraged Neil about the healing power of God as a result of Christ's death on the cross and His resurrection. I constantly quoted to Neil the scripture that states that by the stripes of Jesus we are healed. I don't know what to think now. What can I put my faith in? I have dedicated my whole life to God, only to find there is nothing solid for me to stand on anymore. However, I will not turn from God. I won't, I can't, no matter the circumstances.

In preparation for the funeral, I have been listening to Neil's favourite songs and looking through our photos. I am reminded of how good looking he was and how much we did and enjoyed in the time we were together. We would have been married for fourteen years next month. I don't know how I am going to live without him. I see him everywhere; everything has a memory attached to it. His toothbrush still lays beside mine, and the last two nights have been the first time I have not been by Neil's side, having slept in every uncomfortable hospital chair every night that he was in hospital. I miss him terribly, to the point that I can hardly breathe. This was never supposed to happen; we were supposed to grow old together. So much of my life was wrapped up in my life with Neil. I never wanted to be on my own again.

Lord, where are You?

25 April 2009

I am sitting alone on Anzac Day, watching the most amazing, inspiring, elderly people march to celebrate and remember what they and others have sacrificed for their country and its people, and I envy them because they were given the opportunity to reach old age, something Neil will never do. I am reminded, however, that many, many brave young men died in muddy, filthy and bloody trenches and on foreign beaches and in lonely landscapes. Neil died lying on the bed he picked out when we got married with his father by his side and his wife running around madly, trying her hardest to keep him here.

I have realised in recent days that even though I encouraged

Neil by saying that God is never late and is always on time, because His timing is perfect, and his healing would come, it appears to me now that Neil's death, instead, was in perfect timing. As it would happen, on the afternoon of Neil's death, the girls were not home as they were every other day and were; therefore, spared from seeing the paramedics working to revive Neil after he stopped breathing. Further, his much-loved father had only returned two days previously and was there when Neil took his last breath. With my college classes resuming in three months, I also have time to get my head together to resume study. All of this does little to help ease my pain because I wonder why with all the effort God went to to accommodate Neil's passing and our grief, He didn't just heal Neil instead. I feel like I have been set up. I have lost my husband and I happen to be halfway through a college degree, which I can focus on and it can give me a purpose and a future income. Nothing has been left undone for me, and even though, deep down, I know it is because God is still by my side and His love and blessings surround me, it is cold comfort when I consider what I have lost. What have I lost? I hardly know. Even after three weeks, I don't think I fully understand that he is gone. However, intermittent clarity, like a flickering light, reminds me that I have lost the man who I thought I would grow old with. In quiet times, when I allow myself to think on what has happened, the thought that continually comes to mind is that I am alone in the world. I know that that is not the case; God is with me, my children are my constant companions, and my family, my church family and my friends are never far away. But it's not the same. Neil and I had built a life together, and now I feel that that life has been stripped from me. Where do I go from here? The path I am on is no longer lit. My future is so uncertain.

In the last few weeks, since Neil's death, I have tortured myself. Had I known he was so close to death, I would have done more. It is likely he did have an infection, and, had I been more aware of the situation, he could still be here. However, actions different to the ones taken could have led to him dying alone in an ambulance or a hospital corridor or room. I am resolved now to think that if God, the creator of the universe, wanted Neil to be here, he would be here.

Neil's funeral was beautiful, and his many, many friends came, with some speaking of the positive influence Neil had on their lives. Neil had, in his short life, influenced many people, with one friend saying that Neil had, from a young age, been his 'moral compass.' He was a good man and the cards I have received from his customers help to confirm that.

I do not know how I am going to get through this; I feel the pain so strongly. Friends remind me that it has only been a few short weeks since Neil's death. I guess time will help, I hope so because everything has become dull, tasteless and pointless. Neil laboured in his breathing towards the end and when I lay at night on my own, I hold my breath and imagine how Neil must have felt as he lay there desperate for oxygen. I wonder if I did it for long enough, would I also be free of the pain I feel. I am so tortured. Please help me, Lord. Strengthen me for the journey ahead.

I am told often that I did an excellent job of caring for Neil during his illness. I would have done anything for him, and I just wish I still had the opportunity to care for him. I miss his touch. I miss him lightly tapping my leg through the night to wake me so I can help him go to the toilet. I still have his toothbrush lying beside mine. For many years, we had this unsaid agreement that whoever brushed their teeth first would put paste on the other's toothbrush for them. I cannot stand the thought of throwing it away. I know it is a silly, old toothbrush, but it signifies so much. I handed him that toothbrush twice a day and helped him brush his teeth. Unfortunately, such images and private moments will eventually fade away and become a distant memory. We are here and then we are gone. However, Neil's influence will go on affecting the lives of many; his life will bring glory to God.

24 June 2009

It has been a considerable time since I have written. To write about how I feel and how the girls and I are coping would be to acknowledge reality, the reality being that Neil is gone and I didn't just dream the last five months. Shock and denial have been my friends. It appears that the loss and stress I have experienced is too great a burden, for my mind cannot dwell on it for longer than five to ten minutes a day. When I look back over those terrible three months at the height of Neil's illness, I cannot believe that both Neil and I endured it. Such pain, loss and disappointment. A loss of hope! All hope died when Neil passed away, and now I am left to wonder.

Neil's toothbrush still lays beside mine after almost three months (On Monday, it will be twelve weeks since Neil died). It has gained a layer of dust and is a constant reminder of my loss. It is no longer used daily. Instead, it tells me that I had a husband once and I lost him.

I have progressed enough through my journey of grief to become angry at my situation. Even though I am stable financially due to some insurance and superannuation being paid out, it does not go close to alleviating my pain. I would rather be poor and have Neil still here. However, I should not begrudge God's blessings and provision.

I have started to taste loneliness, even though I am quite independent and strong. I am starting to think and feel that I do not want to be alone. However, at the same time, I do not want to replace Neil. Why is it that no matter how much you want something, you cannot have it? I tried so hard to keep Neil here, but I lost. I am having a dreadful time trying to reconcile the fact that God didn't rescue us like I believed He would. I am heartbroken that Neil is gone. I miss him terribly. I cannot, at the moment, recover from the devastation I feel at being let down by the God in whom I have trusted implicitly most of my life. I cannot read scriptures that promise healing and deliverance without feeling that I am having salt rubbed into open wounds. If you don't believe some of the Bible, you can't stand on any of it. It is all or nothing. And at the moment, I don't know what to believe. Does anyone get healed these days? I have wondered if our lifestyles, which are so influenced by the world, are not conducive to the workings of the miracle-working power of God. Is there too much of the world and not enough of God's power in our lives?

I am still very busy, to keep myself from reality. College starts in approximately four to five weeks. I am concerned that I will not cope, as I have not navigated far through the grieving process.

I have been working on the last painting that Neil saw me paint. I am keeping this one for that reason.

The girls are okay. Shirley has just taken Maya and Callie to Taree for two weeks (It is so quiet!). And Em was filmed today for a game show to be aired on TV. She lost but had lots of fun.

In looking for feel-good moments, I have been to see the movie *The Proposal* almost every day this week! I have accumulated a number of feel-good movies to watch. As the shock wears off, the reality starts to sink in, and I find it difficult to cope. I get anxious, short of breath, agoraphobic and a little bewildered. Going to church without Neil would certainly highlight reality for me, so I have not gone back yet, although I have started considering it.

I spend time with God in worship whilst I paint and when I walk. I will not turn my back on God. He is my life. To turn my back on God would be to turn my back on myself. I will reconcile one hundred percent to God eventually. All that really matters are the eternal things. And as a result of Neil's life of influence and his death, I have become determined to make a difference in this world. Only eternal things matter.

Lord, where are You?

I have just had a glance over journal entries written whilst Neil was in hospital. They highlight the faith that I had and the trust that I had in my God. So, what went wrong?

Lord, You had better be there!

19 January 2010
Well, looking at the last date of entry in this journal, it is apparent that I have not put pen to paper for over six months. How could I write about something that I could not face? A lot has happened to

me in this time. I have literally been in hell and am now starting to see some light. My new motto has become 'I know what pain is, but I also know what love is, and God's love never fails.' Despite the unbearable pain, God has never left my side. He continues to meet my every need. I started back at college in July, and, therefore, commenced one of the most difficult journeys. The stress of study (six units!) mixed with the seeping in of reality almost brought me undone. I spent many nights lying prostrate on the floor begging God for the strength to face the next day, especially during my practicum where I had to teach for four weeks in a school. But I know first-hand that when you are in the depths of darkness, that is where the richest blessings are found. I was incredibly blessed in my prac placement, blessed by both the staff and the students. In my last lesson, I shared my testimony through tears with my Year 9 History class. I spoke to them about how even in dark times they are never alone; God is with them. I told them that if they remembered in five or ten years anything that I taught them about Indigenous History, I would be happy, but what was far more important was remembering that they can call on God in their time of need. Some of the students were crying and both the students and I were blessed as God did His work. To be used by God has always been my greatest desire, so I feel incredibly blessed by the whole experience. It appears that people want to listen to you when you experience pain and tragedy. Not long after that prac, my dad started to lose his own battle with cancer. I raced down to Tuncurry to say goodbye, and he passed away later that day, on 14 November, 2009, which was at the height of my college assessments and exams. After months of 'coping' and holding it together, I started to come undone. And the day before my final exam, I was incapable of controlling my emotions and managed to stop just short of insanity and hysterics. Praise God for a few extremely supportive friends who prayed for me. Because of their support, I was able to sit the exam and finish the semester. As I sat in the exam room, close to tears because I had just lost my father seven months after losing my husband, I knew that in that moment I was covered in prayer. In fact, one of my lecturers came to sit in on the start of the exam to see if I was okay. He didn't leave until I managed, after some time, to pick up my pen and start writing. I was so blessed by his care and support.

However, as my life has rarely known peace, it is no surprise that I had more and still more to face. Just before travelling down to Taree for Christmas, I was told that Maya had a rather alarming 'lesion' on her eye and now she needs to see a specialist. That appointment is this Friday, and I am so scared because I cannot cope with any more bad news. How on earth would I cope with a serious situation in Maya's health again on my own without Neil? I can't help but wonder if these are my last days of sanity before I receive more news that will send me into utter and total despair. I am trying to put my faith and trust in God, but because of my disappointment over unanswered prayers for Neil, I feel like I am simply nailing jelly to a tree. I have very little to pin my faith on at the moment. However, God is my God and the King of my life and He will do His will and I will trust in His purpose, love and power. [Dear reader, this situation with Maya's health ended positively; it was just a benign discolouration. Praise God!]

Over Christmas, I faced a lot of my fears and started to face reality. It was my first Christmas without Neil, on my own. The girls and I managed, and whilst there at the Tyrie farm, we all dealt with Neil's ashes, creating a memorial under a tree in his parents' beautiful garden—pain and suffering. However, I am back home and, having turned a corner, I attended my first Sunday morning service last week, and I managed not to shed a tear. Tomorrow is my first birthday on my own, without Neil. Lord, help me and provide me with strength and peace tomorrow. I still love You and I *always* will.

ONLY ETERNAL THINGS MATTER!

PS. Last week, I was finally able to throw away Neil's toothbrush after nine and a half months.

Chapter Sixteen

AFTER THE STORM

*'What lies behind us and what lies ahead of us are
tiny matters compared to what lives within us'*

Henry David Thoreau

A t the funeral, I told my college lecturers that if I could string more than two words together by the time the next semester came around, I would be back. I gave myself three months to gather myself together before going back to college full time, in fact, more than full time. Other universities had four units of work per semester. We had five. I chose to do six. I wanted to make up lost time for the semester that I had deferred. As far as I was concerned, my life had been robbed enough. I was going to finish as close to the original time as possible. That did not mean that I had recovered from Neil's passing, far from it. It just meant that I had something to distract me so that I could not think about it.

I worked very hard across all subjects, achieving top marks. I enjoyed learning again, and I was so grateful that, even though my world had been turned upside down, there was something that was certain. I did not have to contemplate what I was going to do as a single mother and the one provider for my family; I was halfway through a Bachelor degree. I often wondered if God placed that burning desire for me to go to uni way back then, knowing how much of a lifeline it would be for me years later. The college staff were extremely supportive, to say the least, and over the two years that I was there after Neil's death, some of the lecturers practically begged me to take extensions for my assessment tasks; I generally declined the offer, wanting to get them out of the way. I did very well on my practicums and was loved by most of my students, and with such a high GPA, I was on the Dean's Honour List.

However, despite my best efforts, it was impossible for me to finish with the rest of my cohort. I had missed a prac placement and I could only do one a semester. So, after my cohort finished in November 2010, I remained to finish my degree. I finally reached that goal in April 2011 when I completed a six-week teaching internship. As I drove away from the school on the last day of my internship, I spent a moment talking to Neil, who, in five days' time, would have been gone for two years. I told him through tears that I had finally done it; I had gotten my degree. Only God and I knew just how difficult that had been, having spent the first two years juggling my degree whilst my husband battled cancer and then for the last two years doing it on my own while caring for three children and grieving my loss. Some nights, after I came home from teaching on my prac, I laid on the floor in my bedroom and cried till I had no more tears left. In those moments, I had no idea how I was going to get through the next day, teaching up to 150 students. I stayed on the floor until I felt the strength of God permeate my being. Once refreshed and renewed in my faith, knowing that God would go before me, I got off the floor and began the hours and hours of planning that lay ahead of me before I could finally go to sleep in the wee hours of the morning. The stress and pressure were so great, and I was still so vulnerable, not that I let on to anybody. I was a survivor; I always had been. It was what I did best: survive.

The most difficult time in that season was when I received the call from my family to tell me that my dad was dying after struggling with his own cancer battle. Despite my dad's troubles and vices, I had worked hard to build a good relationship with him, and I had encouraged him over the years in his own journey with God, having found God when in rehab. Neil had only been gone for seven months and the thought of watching another loved one die in front of me was almost more than I could bear. I decided to drive down to see my dad on his deathbed, and after he passed away on 14 November 2009, I spoke at his funeral. It was important for me to honour Dad's life and tell family and friends that he had a relationship with God. His friends would benefit from hearing about the hope that came from knowing God. Even though it was extremely difficult to compose myself enough to speak, I was not losing the opportunity to bring God into the picture. Standing before the crowd of family and friends, I said:

'Today we are here to farewell and send off my father, Trevor John Hardy. My dad was a character, to say the least, and as a result he endeared himself to many.

'Those who knew my father knew that he had his personal demons, alcohol being a thorn in his side. This got him into a lot of trouble over the years; however, it cannot be denied that Dad always tried to act with good intentions. He was always looking for an opportunity to help somebody in need. He tried hard over the years to separate himself from the drink, but it was a battle he couldn't win.

'My grandmother brought Dad up to believe in God and read the Bible, and when Dad was in rehab in Queensland, he encountered God. He would often tell me about how he would pray to God every evening whilst he battled his illness.

'In one phone conversation we had, he was telling me about how he liked being in Sydney for treatment because nobody knew his reputation or his past. I said to Dad, 'You know, Dad, when you ask God to forgive your sins, he doesn't remember them anymore.' He replied, 'I know that, darlin', it's the other bloody bastards that I am worried about!' [At this point, reader, I turned and apologised to the Archdeacon who took the service whilst the audience chuckled.]

'Dad had his weaknesses, but don't we all? None of us are

perfect. Dad knew that God loved him despite those weaknesses. The Bible says that Jesus came to save sinners, not saints, and we are all sinners in this place today. Dad found peace in God during his last trying months. If you are experiencing trials or are lacking peace in your life, there is no place too dark where God cannot find you. I have experienced this personally, having lost my own husband to cancer only seven months ago. Despite my pain and suffering, I am never alone. Despite my trials, I am blessed. Who will you call on in your time of need? I can say that a life without God is no life; it is simply going through the motions. Today, my dad experiences peace in the arms of God because he put his trust in Him. I experience peace amidst my loss because I put my trust in God. And today, as we remember the father, brother, uncle, grandfather, nephew, cousin, and friend that we have lost, I encourage you to do the same. I would like to leave you with a scripture that has given me great comfort at times like this. It is Psalm 121:

I WILL lift up my eyes to the hills— From whence comes my help?
My help comes from the Lord, Who made heaven and earth.
He will not allow your foot to be moved; He who keeps you will not slumber.
Behold, He who keeps Israel Shall neither slumber nor sleep. The LORD is your keeper;
The LORD is your shade at your right hand. The sun shall not strike you by day,
Nor the moon by night.
The LORD shall preserve you from all evil; He shall preserve your soul.
The LORD shall preserve your going out and your coming in
From this time forth, and even forevermore. (NKJV)'

The day after returning from Dad's funeral, I had to sit exams for college. The pressure of everything got on top of me and I had come undone. I was unable to compose myself, crying and sobbing uncontrollably. I became so scared because, despite all I had been through, it was the first time that I had no control over myself. At first, I could not get it together enough to study for my exam, but I was able to rely on the prayers of a few people that I trusted and was able to sit the exam, knowing that I was covered in prayer. It was just another time that I had to step up and push through, using every bit of resolve that I could muster, relying on God for the strength that I did not possess.

I now look back at my time at Christian Heritage College and see it as being very blessed. The staff and fellow students were such a blessing to me, and I have thanked God numerous times for bringing such wonderful, encouraging, and supportive people into my life.

Chapter Seventeen

RESOLUTION

*'Evening and morning and at noon I will pray, and
cry aloud. And He shall hear my voice.*
*He has redeemed my soul in peace from
the battle that was against me'*

Psalm 55:17-18 (NKJV)

....●

A s I sit and write this chapter, it is July 2012, and it has been
three years and six months since Neil's death. I am trying
to put into words how I survived that time and how I can sit
here now mostly healed and restored with my faith not only intact,
but strengthened and developed. The challenge for me now is to
communicate in the physical what has happened to me emotionally
and spiritually. This is the part of the book that aligns with its
purpose: to encourage and inspire, to communicate the depth and
breadth of God's love and faithfulness, and to communicate that
there is no place dark enough where God's light cannot shine.

In the beginning, as previously stated, I struggled with being
forsaken by my loving Heavenly Father. However, as before, when
I made the vow to God to not turn my back on Him if Maya did not
make it, I held the same conviction. I was not turning my back on
God even though my husband died. I never actually got to a place in

Neil's battle where I voiced out loud to God my vow as I did with Maya's battle. To be honest, I was not sure if it was a commitment that I could hold to, plus, as far as I was concerned, he was not going anywhere. One needs to understand the difference between the possibility of losing a child and the possibility of losing a spouse to fully understand where I was at. Having almost lost one of my children, I can only guess at the absolute heartbreak of actually losing one. I am so grateful that I was spared this, having witnessed personally the devastation experienced by parents at Ronald McDonald House who lost their precious children. However, when you lose a child, if circumstances allow, you are supported by your spouse; it is something you go through together. However, when you lose your spouse, you are left alone, and not only that, but you lose half of yourself. The Bible states that when a man and a woman come together, they become one flesh (Genesis 2:24). I fully experienced the pain of losing half of myself, losing the person who knew me better than anyone, the one person who I had been intimate with, the one person who promised to stay with me for life. Yes, the love of family, friends, and my church family softened the blow, but nothing replaces that relationship when it is gone. I had people try to comfort me by telling me of the loss of their relatives, siblings, and so forth. It's heart-breaking and tragic, but it's not the same. I felt lost, unanchored, like I was drifting for months in a fog, mentally, emotionally and spiritually.

I think what affected me the most in the first few days, weeks, and months was noticing the loss of the covering that I had as a wife. When you are married, you belong to somebody. When you go out into the world, walking around the shops, attending events and so forth, even if you are alone physically, you are not really alone; there is someone who cares for you, someone you can call on anytime for help and support, someone who will pick up a loaf of bread on their way home from work because you asked them to. Once Neil was gone, I felt exposed, alone, on display even. I had belonged to one man for nearly fourteen years—longer if you count our courtship and engagement—and now I was on my own, up for grabs, so to speak. I found that very difficult, and, to be honest, I have struggled with it ever since. I had never thought I would be in this place again—on the market and available—and I became very defensive and scared. I now walk into rooms on my own, belonging to no one. Yes, I am never really alone because my girls often trail behind me, but it is not the same. And, of course, I am never alone any minute of the day or night because my God never leaves me nor forsakes me (Hebrews 13:5). However, at the time, I struggled. Now, I have gotten to a place in my life where my relationship with God is enough; in fact, it is more than enough. He has become my constant companion, the one in whom I can place all my trust, my hope, and my faith. He knows what is going on in my heart without me having to tell Him. It is a true romance between my Creator and me. He provides for me and meets my needs, always having my best interests at heart, and all He asks for is my complete devotion.

Even though I chose not to turn my back on my relationship with God, I did not go back to church for almost a year after Neil passed away. There were a few reasons for this. Firstly, this was Neil's and my church where we had been fed spiritually for eight years before he passed away. Some of the people in the church had known Neil longer than I had. I could not face going back there without him. Secondly, it was where the funeral was held, and being in the throes of grief and subsequent denial, the last thing I wanted was to go back to where the casket had sat that day. It was the last place that I saw Neil in the physical world. However, the biggest reason why I chose to stay away from church was that my battle with grief was a battle between me and God. I wanted to hear what He had to say about what did and did not happen, not what man had to say. I really did not want people's opinions about why Neil was not healed; mind you, I did not avoid such declarations completely. I just wanted to rest in God and allow Him to heal me and restore my heart and spirit back to health. Having a hiatus from church is not something that I would recommend for others in a similar position to me, as the fellowship of the saints is vitally important for spiritual, mental, and emotional health. Even though I was not in the church physically, my heart was still there. Members of my church family visited me often, and my pastors knew my heart and supported me, letting me know that the church family was waiting to welcome me back when I felt the time was right. One of my few concerns was that my girls were not going to church regularly; however, they were also supported. I was also concerned that the young people who I mentored would view my sabbatical as evidence of a loss of faith on my part. Eventually, they came to see that my relationship with God was strengthened as He became my healer, my comforter, and my closest friend.

Music had always had a powerful effect on me, and in my grief, this worked in a good and bad way. I knew that I would lose all composure if I stood in my church, participating in worship. At home, whilst I tried to connect with God after Neil's death, worship was both beautiful and bitter at the same time. The words spoke of a God who healed, a God who answered prayers. The praise songs spoke of 'happy days' and the need for dancing because of God's goodness. To me, it was like rubbing salt into a very open and exposed wound. However, worship was always the way that I connected with my Heavenly Father, how I allowed the Holy Spirit to come and minister to me, so I persisted, a little bit at a time. I would lie by myself on the floor, the lounge, the bed, and just let the worship flow over me. I allowed the Holy Spirit to minister to me and heal me. Through tears, I cried out to my God, offering Him my shattered heart. I cried out to the God who had allowed me to go through so many struggles, who had seemingly forsaken me. He met with me every time. His presence was like a sweet-smelling balm that gently healed my heart, never invading, never causing additional pain, but revealing His love for me in a way that allowed me to hope. Over time, that flickering light from the lighthouse got brighter and became more constant, and I could breathe again.

Shortly after returning to college, someone finally had the courage to ask me how I was going with it all. Not many people did. I spoke of similar things to those outlined in this book, and then, as I sat there, the person told me something that brought instant revelation to me in a way that allowed me to see God in every frame of the time that Neil had battled cancer and subsequently lost the battle. They explained to me that a one-off healing, the kind that I had been expecting in faith from God, was like God coming and dropping a basket of assistance at my front door and not coming back. However, sometimes God worked differently; instead of getting that one basket containing that one-off healing, God came every single day and left with me everything that I needed to get through that day. The person went on to explain that in doing so, God showed a constant and repeated love and care not seen in the first option. In that moment, I was able to put God into the picture because even though I did not get what I wanted—Neil's healing—I could not deny that God was there each and every day giving me what I needed to get through the trial. This meant a lot to me; He *was* there. I saw His hand at work in many things. I no longer felt in my heart the way that I had that first night that I found myself alone on that bed. I no longer felt forsaken. He was there all along.

Perhaps the thing that caused me the greatest amount of heartache with regards to Neil's death was not, in fact, his death, but the way he died, his last days with us. I felt sorry for Neil and thought that it was very unfair. From the time of his stroke, he was reduced to a person so unlike his normal self. In fact, when he died, I grieved for two Neils. I grieved for the one to whom I had been married for all those years, the funny, teasing, witty, competent, and self-sufficient one. And I grieved for the Neil who was the broken man, who was totally reliant on me for everything, who sat quietly and reflected in his own little world. I felt that Neil deserved more than the ending he had been given. He would try to read his beloved Bible, but he could not even do that. He was a man who was great with his hands, able to fix anything, things that professionals had long since given up on, and he loved to speak about God to everyone he met. Yet, he was reduced to sitting in his chair, unable to use one arm, unable to speak, and barely able to walk. He was an independent man who had been a bachelor for so long, and, at the end of his life, he could not even feed or bathe himself.

I also felt extremely robbed because in those last three months, after the stroke, I was not able to have a conversation with him. Other couples facing terminal illness are generally given the time together that becomes so precious, when things are said and trips are taken. However, my husband of nearly fourteen years could not and did not even say goodbye to me. Further, he was stripped of the opportunity to say goodbye to his three girls who he adored, leaving them without communicating messages that would comfort them in the years to come. We were left with nothing, and Neil did not get to say what was on his heart. That broke me more than anything. In trying to come to some resolution with that, I wondered if Neil had been brought to that place of total dependence so that his last days here were spent in humble stillness before his God. I thought maybe it was God's way of getting Neil ready for his entrance into the Kingdom of God, going in, not in his own strength or ability, but resting solely on the grace of God. It's a beautiful thought because there is no safer place to be than being fully reliant on God.

At some point, unknown to me, he would have realised that his time was up, and I never knew. I never knew what he was thinking or how he was feeling. I tried to work it out, but I could only hazard a guess. Most of the time, he was upbeat, smiling, and pushing through his limitations.

But what has stayed with me and caused me considerable pain are the moments when he would cry, sobbing, my strong and independent husband, and I had no idea why. I asked myself many times, what was he thinking? In those moments, I tried to calm him and encourage him. I remember saying to him, 'Hey, don't you give up on me! I am not giving up! God is still on the throne and He will deliver us.' I don't think, however, that he ever gave up on God; rather, he gave up on wanting to be here. His sights were set on where he really wanted to be. At the wake, I was telling some people that when Neil was in distress, lying on the bed just before he died, he was looking out the large bedroom window at the clear, blue Autumn sky. I explained that he never took his eyes off the sky despite his discomfort. Neil's dad was beside me during the conversation and he said that he had noticed the same thing when

I was ringing the ambulance and when he sat with Neil in his final moments. Not once did he take his eyes off that blue sky. I may not have been able to ascertain much of what was going through Neil's mind during those final months, but I am certain that Neil's final thoughts were focused on where he knew he was going: to rest in the arms of his Saviour.

After his stroke, Neil sometimes sat in his chair and watched Christian music video clips. I can vividly remember him listening to one particular song by one of his favourite Christian bands, Leeland, which speaks about the tears of the saints who cry out for those who are lost and separated from God. He sat there in his chair, crying. Even though he was unable to speak, he still communicated to us the love that he still had for his God and the hunger he still had to see people saved and coming into a right relationship with their Creator. The poem I wrote to go on Neil's memorial stone sums up the hope we have in knowing that Neil died with his faith intact:

'You are no longer here; you are in the arms of Jesus, But we will not fear, for our faith will reunite us.'

Knowing that we will meet up with Neil again one day has given the girls and me considerable comfort.

Chapter Eighteen

HEALING COMES

'He heals the brokenhearted And binds up their wounds'

Psalm 147:3 (NKJV)

....●

There have been many revelations and moments that have seen me step one foot in front of the other towards the healing that has restored me today. Although, I won't sugar coat it; there is still much work to do, for me and for my girls. However, what I have learnt is that grief is a bizarre thing; it is something that you have no control over, really. In the very beginning, after Neil died, my brain was in total denial, perhaps shock. Once, when I used to minister in a nursing home, a lovely elderly woman told me that her daughter had died two years before in a car accident. She went on to say that in those two years, after her daughter's death, she could not remember her daughter at all, including what she looked like. At the time, I was very surprised and perplexed, but I now understand what she was experiencing. While I did remember who Neil was and what he looked like, any time I tried to think about him, I actually couldn't. It was like my brain would shut off completely and would not allow me to visit that part of my life; it was too difficult. My brain knew that the pain was too great; it simply would not let me go there. So, in the first few months, I had to force myself to think about Neil and our life together. Eventually, the time spent dwelling on

Neil, before my brain decided that that was enough, got longer and longer. Once a month, Neil's former work truck would come into our street to pick up garden bags, and I would force myself to look at it. I would tell myself: 'Look! That was Neil's truck. You know— Neil. *Your* Neil.' The truck was still the same colour that Neil had so proudly painted, and it still had the sign that he designed and had made. My mind and my heart just did not want to go there. So, I came to the conclusion that I could not force the grieving process to move any faster than it did. I certainly cried a lot. I reached a milestone after five or so months when I actually got through a day without shedding a tear. It was the little things that signalled reality for me: songs on the radio that Neil and I loved, movies that we had seen together, or in one case, learning that his favourite shop, Aldi, was opening down the road from us.

As expected, the difficult days were the anniversaries, the firsts of everything. The first week, the first month, the first year, the first birthdays, the first wedding anniversary, the first Christmas, the first Easter, and the first dance comp the girls went to without their dad. Each time, I felt that the girls and I had been robbed. On the first-year anniversary of Neil's death, I was still, even then, finding it difficult to come to terms with reality; it almost felt like Neil was just on a very extended holiday. So, I watched the film *PS. I Love You,* which, surprisingly, was very accurate at depicting what my life had been like for the last year. I was able to point out the moments that I, myself, had experienced as a widow losing her young husband to cancer. To say I shed a lot of tears would be a gross understatement. As part of my grieving process, it is a movie that I still watch occasionally to help me to come to terms with the fact that Neil is not coming back. It forces me to deal with reality. However, dear reader, I have not run off with a cute Irishman . . . yet!

Perhaps the most significant moment that steered me towards healing was when I was at a self-improvement and leadership seminar in the US in 2011. I was encouraged, along with the rest of the participants, to imagine myself on my own deathbed, looking back on my life. I was to envision myself walking towards Heaven as my breath slipped away, having said goodbye to all those I loved. In that moment, unexpectedly, the most incredible wave of love and peace enveloped me. I knew instantly, at my core, that it was the divine love of the Creator of the universe. It was certainly not of this world and the peace I felt could not be described with words. I have not experienced anything like it before or since, and I truly believe it was my Heavenly Daddy opening my eyes to a glimpse of eternal joy and peace. In that very moment, I was released from the struggle of remembering Neil's final moments. I thought to myself, 'Oh my goodness! If this is what Neil experienced when he walked towards his Saviour, I am okay with it. I am okay with it.' All I had seen from my end when Neil was dying was the chaos, the commotion, and Neil's laboured breathing. However, for a brief moment, I got a glimpse of what Neil would have experienced in that moment: an unconditional, everlasting love and perfect peace. He had finally reached the destination that he had been preparing for his whole life. It released me, and, finally, I was free to walk forward, no longer feeling sorry for Neil or being tormented by his final moments here. The Bible says, 'So when this corruptible has put on incorruption, and this mortal has put on immortality, then shall be brought to pass the saying that is written: *"Death is swallowed up in victory." O Death, where is your sting?"* '(1 Corinthians 15:54-55, NKJV) This speaks of the sting of death being overthrown by the death of Christ on the cross and His resurrection, our hope that leads to eternal life.

Our life here is only the introduction to our final destination. Like Queen Esther in the Bible who was prepared to go before the king to be taken as his wife, prepared with sweet-smelling oils and perfumes (Esther 2:12), so we are prepared and made ready for our entrance to stand before the one who bought us with a price, the price of God's Son on the cross (1 Corinthians 6:20; Colossians 1:19-21). Our life does not end when we leave here; it is only just beginning. What we do here prepares us for our grand entrance into eternity.

It did not take long for me to realise after Neil's death that only eternal things really matter, and as a result, I have been on a quest to make a difference while I am here on this earth. None of us know how long we will be here, and like Neil, I want to do as much as I can to extend the Kingdom of God while I am here, to be a blessing to others and to communicate the Truth of God's Word. In a sense, I am ruined forever; I will never be satisfied with a nine-to-five job or with mediocrity or complacency. I now have a burning desire to speak of God's goodness, His faithfulness, and the hope that He alone can bring. My God was able to get me through the most difficult times in my life, when it was so dark, so overwhelming, and so horrendous. He deserves one hundred percent of my time and devotion; my life is His. When one experiences the saving grace of God time and time again as I have, nothing else even comes close to being of importance. He saved me. It is as simple as that, and He saves me every day, every single day.

I have been asked many times how I got through everything that I have endured, and it is really difficult for me to pinpoint every single thing that happened to bring about my healing and restoration. One answer I give is 'Knowing where to get my strength from, and knowing that it does not come from me, but God.' But, ultimately, I have endured because of my hope in a faithful God.

Chapter Nineteen

THE DIFFERENCE

Take a good look at God's wonders...
they'll take your breath away.
He converted sea to dry land; travelers crossed the
river on foot. Now isn't that cause for a song?

Psalm 66:5 (MSG)

....●

There is a song that I hear on the radio by the band, Fire Flight. The song is called 'For Those Who Wait', and it speaks to me about what I have gained out of my experiences. One line in particular stands out. It says, 'The hard lessons make the difference and the difference makes it worth it.' I know this to be true in my own life. All of my experiences have helped to mould me into a vessel that God can use. As hard as it is to recognise the necessity of my trials, I would prefer to have gone through my life experiences so that I may be a worthier vessel rather than stay as I was. Although, at no time would I ever choose to lose Neil for any gain on my part nor propose that it was God's will to take Neil for such a gain.

Even though I was a relatively normal person in the eyes of most, there were things in my life that held me back and caused me to view things in an incorrect light. I had pride, unforgiveness, fear, self-centredness, anger, and a myriad of other things plaguing my life before I went through the fires of trial. My favourite scripture since my teenage years has always been, '*When* He has tested me, I shall come forth as gold.' (Job 23:10, NKJV) I have been through the fire of testing and my character has been refined and strengthened. This is important to me because my character determines whether or not I can sustain my gifts and abilities and fulfil my purpose in God. In each trial that I faced, there was something that I could take away to help me endure the next; such is the faithfulness of God to equip me during my trials that I may come out each time more beautiful, purer, and closer to Him.

Just because my life had taken an unexpected detour did not mean that I was on the wrong path. Nothing happens apart from God's will. And even if we would prefer to be anywhere else than where we are when enduring trials, it is far better to be where we are than anywhere else because in that place God's will can be perfected in our lives. Were Shadrach, Meshach and Abednego on the wrong path when they faced the fiery furnace? No, they were exactly where they were supposed to be. They stood firm in their faith, refusing to bow down to King Nebuchadnezzar, saying to him: 'If we are thrown into the blazing furnace, the God we serve is able to deliver us from it, and he will deliver us from Your majesty's hand. *But even if he does not . . .*' (Daniel 3:17-18, NIV). God allowed them to be thrown into the furnace and they still went in with their faith intact. But God was right there with them in the flames: 'Look! I see four men walking around in the fire, unbound and unharmed' (Daniel 3:25, NIV), and when the men came out unscathed, with not one hair singed, they did not even smell of smoke. God saw the bigger picture. He knows the end from the beginning. He *will* deliver us, but it may not be in the way we want; however, it will be in a way that aligns with the greater purposes that we don't yet see: 'Then Nebuchadnezzar said, "Praise be to the God of Shadrach, Meshach and Abednego, who has sent his angel and rescued his servants! (Daniel 3:28, NIV) The king went on to decree that anyone who spoke against the God of Shadrach, Meshach and Abednego would be punished with death, and the three men were promoted in the province of Babylon. We cannot view our circumstances through the lens of our earthly limitations. God *is* God, and we are called to rest and trust in His sovereignty, regardless of the circumstances. Ultimately, the men were perfected in their faith and promoted, having endured the fiery trial, and God was glorified.

Further, James 1:2-4 speaks of the value of experiencing trials, saying, 'My brethren, count it all joy when you fall into various trials, knowing that the testing of your faith produces patience. But let patience have *its* perfect work, that you may be perfect and complete, lacking nothing.' (NKJV) I would certainly prefer to be lacking nothing, having endured trials, than live a comfortable life that is wanting and separated from God. It is through trials that we grow the most; the fire refines us and burns away the dross. Proverbs 25:4-5 says, 'Remove impurities from the silver and the silversmith can craft a fine chalice.' (MSG) More than anything, I want to be a chalice that God can use.

We all endure seasons of trials in our lives. The key is in knowing that there is a purpose and reason for every season. We are to endure, knowing that there is a bigger picture than the pain we are currently experiencing and that we can trust God to do His work for our benefit and His glory. Ecclesiastes 3:1 says, 'To everything *there is* a season, A time for every purpose under heaven.' (NKJV) There will be dark seasons in our lives, but the bitter-cold seasons will end and spring will come. To mix metaphors: after the night comes the dawn—the dawn comes every day. Psalm 30:5 says, 'Weeping may endure for a night, But joy *comes* in the morning.' (NKJV) The Bible tells us that an easy life is not promised to those who love God but perseverance during trials brings forth its reward. The winter makes the spring more beautiful. One Peter 1:6-7 says, 'In this you greatly rejoice, though now for a little while, if need be, you have been grieved by various trials, that the genuineness of your faith, *being* much more precious than gold that perishes, though it is tested by fire, may be found to praise, honor and glory at the revelation of Jesus Christ.' (NKJV)

Even though we are not exempt from trials, there are things that are promised to us as children of God that will sustain us: the promise that we are never alone (Hebrews 13:5), that God's love never fails us (1 Corinthians 13:8), that we will not be given more than we can handle (1 Corinthians 10:13), and that ultimately, we win, receiving redemption, salvation, and eternal life through the blood of Christ (Ephesians 1:7; 1 Thessalonians 5:9; John 3:16). I have been encouraged recently by the scripture in Revelation 7:13-17, which speaks of the end days and their tribulation. Despite this context, it has provided me with great comfort with regards to the trials that I have faced in my life:

Then one of the elders answered, saying to me, 'Who are these arrayed in white robes, and where did they come from?' And I said to him, 'Sir, you know.' So he said to me, 'These are the ones who come out of the great tribulation, and washed their robes and made them white in the blood of the Lamb. Therefore they are before the throne of God, and serve Him day and night in His temple. And He who sits on the throne will dwell among them. They shall neither hunger anymore nor thirst anymore; the sun shall not strike them, nor any heat; for the Lamb who is in the midst of the throne will shepherd them and lead them to living fountains of waters. And God will wipe away every tear from their eyes. (NKJV)

At the time of writing this book, I have been blessed with the amazing privilege of being a guest speaker on numerous occasions in front of many, many young people in schools and churches. When speaking to one group of young people, I had put two rocks into a brown paper bag. I asked an audience member to come out and describe what each of the rocks felt like by putting a hand in the bag. One rock was very smooth and one rock was extremely jagged. I went on to tell the audience that before experiencing the trials that I faced, I was like that jagged rock with bits protruding, sharp and uninviting. I went on to explain that because of what I had endured in my life, I had now become more like the smooth rock, having dealt with those things that were ugly and offensive in my life. I finished my talk by asking the audience the question, 'When you stand before God one day, which rock would you prefer to be like, the jagged rock or the smooth rock?' If one's mind, soul, and spirit are eternity focussed, the answer should be the latter and the trials can be seen for their value.

Further, I recently spoke to a large group of senior students who were about to leave school and go off into the world. I encouraged them to not vote out of the game of life because their circumstances were less than ideal or because they had been robbed in some way by their past experiences. We all have a choice to make about the way we are going to live our lives, and the choice is up to us and us alone. I explained that I could have allowed my experiences to get the better of me and could have given my losses the permission to keep me from living the life that I deserved as a child of the Most High God, but I chose to live in the promises of God. I chose to make the best of what I had, knowing that my God would turn it around for good (Romans 8:28) and that there was a purpose in my suffering. I chose to see the good in the bad. I chose to see the light in the darkness. I chose to see the beauty in the pain.

Nowadays, I make it a part of my daily routine to search out beauty in everything. Every day there is something to be thankful for; His mercies are new every morning (Lamentations 3:22-23). When I walk down to the waterfront of the bay near my home, I am reminded of the awesome power of my God to create such beauty; one flower speaks volumes of the majesty and wonder of God. As I walk, I am often reminded of the scripture that says that the trees of the field will clap their hands (Isaiah 55:12). Even creation recognises the majesty of God. Evidence of God's majesty, power and beauty is everywhere if we choose to see it. The famous artist, Henri Matisse, once said, 'There are always flowers for those who want to see them.' Even in the darkest moments of my life, I have experienced blessings and beheld beauty because I was never ever alone; my God was with me holding my hand, carrying me. A quote by Ralph Waldo Emerson sums up my view of life: 'But in the mud and scum of things, there always, always something sings.' I can honestly say that I feel as if I am the most blessed person on the planet. Sometimes I cannot contain the joy that I feel. It's the joy that comes from being in relationship with God, who takes us by the hand and leads us on an amazing journey of grace, mercy, love, provision, healing, restoration, forgiveness, and salvation. Isaiah 55:12 says, 'For you shall go out with joy, And be led out with peace.' (NKJV) I need not be anxious for anything because my God has never let me down and He never ever will. What a faithful God! What a blessed place to be in: casting all of our cares upon a God who cares for us (1 Peter 5:7).

As I close this chapter and reflect back on my experiences, I am reminded of the word that I received from God at the conference way back in the beginning of Neil's illness: 'This is bigger than both of you. It is for My glory. Everything will be okay. You just need to trust me.' Well, reader, I can honestly say that everything is okay. Such is the power of God to restore and keep us. Such is the power of God to save us through His love for us. The word I received did not return void but spoke Truth, a truth that outworks in my life every day: everything is okay. I now live a blessed life with my girls, who, themselves, are experiencing great blessings. In looking at my girls, I cannot account for why they are doing so well except for the intervention of my loving, faithful God. I am reminded that those who seek first the Kingdom of God and His righteousness have their needs met (Matthew 6:33).

However, I'm not going to lie and say it's perfect or it's easy. The journey has been incredibly hard and it's not over. The girls and I still wear the scars from dealing with the trauma and the loss, and there will be moments where we will need to dig deeper and let God deal with hidden wounds. But to look at Maya, one would never know what she has been through; she is a living testament to the power of God to save and to keep those who belong to Him. Her determination in life will see her achieve her dreams. She walks and speaks very well, and she continually surprises her teachers with her progress. I am blessed to say that all my girls have a love for God and curiously search after Him; how blessed am I. They know that in being in relationship with the God of their father, they will see him again one day. Further, my relationship with my mum and the rest of my family is going from strength to strength and I enjoy the time that I spend with them. My mum has become a great support to me in the last few years, and I am so proud of her. Yes, I am truly blessed, and I am excited about my future, a future that will always be underpinned by the hope that I have in my faithful God.

As I finish writing this book, I contemplate my future. I do not know in detail what it holds for me, but I am certain that God will work in me for His glory. It is my hope that He will use me for 'greater things.' (John 14:12) Due to God's hold on my life, I have struggled with whether teaching is enough in providing me an opportunity to serve my God, and that is all I want to do. God has the answer to this question, and I am assured that He will direct me onto the path that He has faithfully and lovingly prepared for me. You may wonder, dear reader, as you come to the end of the book, whether I have found someone to walk beside my girls and me in life. No, I have not. I told God that I would not consider entering into a relationship with anyone until the second anniversary of Neil's death. That has come and gone. I wait for the one that God has set apart to partner with me in the next part of my journey. I have not always been open to this; in fact, I have been in considerable resistance to it. However, I will not allow my fears to rob the girls and me of the blessings that God has in store for us. It was only six months or so ago that I was in my backyard and my elderly male neighbour, who has hardly spoken more than a few sentences to me in the last eight years, yelled over the fence to me, saying in his thick Yugoslavian accent, 'Now Julie, you need to keep up with da men!' At first, I thought I must have misheard him. I replied, 'Sorry?' and he delivered the same directive. In amusement I told him, 'We'll see.' I rest in knowing that God supplies all my needs and He knows what is best for me. He *is* faithful.

As I close out this topic, this chapter and this book, I am reminded of two scriptures that God has laid on my heart recently that will now underpin my life. They are: 'I *am* my beloved's, And my beloved *is* mine.'(Song of Solomon 6:3, NKJV), and 'I *am* my beloved's, And

His desire *is* toward me.'(Song of Solomon 7:10, NKJV) His love is enough for me and regardless of what the future holds for my girls and me, I have hope in a faithful God who has never failed me, a God who saved me, delivered me, and set me on the path to life everlasting:

Lord, 'You have turned for me my mourning into dancing; You have put off my sackcloth and clothed me with gladness, To the end that *my* glory may sing praise to You and not be silent. O LORD my God, I will give thanks to You forever.' (Psalm 30:11-12, NKJV)

Epilogue

Dear reader, this short story that I wrote, which I believe was inspired by God, represents the woman that I would have become if I allowed the past to rule me, if I allowed the experiences that I went through to rob me of a positive future, and if I had not allowed God to heal me. To me, this is not simply a work of fiction but rather an existent destination that I avoided because I chose to put my life into the hands of my loving God and chose to leave it there... permanently.

The Woman Who Listened to Her Past

The story begins in a darkened room bordered with walls that have become sullied over time. The stained, heavy curtains that cloak the windows push back any evidence of light. A musty smell lingers, and all is quiet. Silence rings out in a deafening blow to the senses till a woman softly pads into the room wearing a garment that disguises her slight frame and constricts her. The folds drop to the ground, heavy and lifeless.

She walks over to the draped windows and parts the dark fabric. As she does, light bursts into the room and highlights the decay. In a sunbeam, particles of dust float aimlessly as light bounces off the woman's silvery hair and continues its mission, defining the lines in her face. In a sweep of her gaze, the woman sees movement, life. Birds are flitting in the overgrown garden. A lizard starts and runs across the moss-covered path and under a thorny hedge. The offending members of the untamed hedge glisten in the sunlight like spears ready to deter invaders.

As the woman stands in front of the dirty pane, faded memories recall gabled country houses lined along the road, nestled in the curves of a field of wildflowers. Time has altered the canvas. Dark green foliage now obscures her view of the outside world as abandonment and neglect encroach upon her.

Unaccustomed to the bright hue of sunlight, she closes the curtains. The room falls back into its ominous shade of gloom. Once the woman's eyes adjust to the familiar darkness, she glances around the small room that once welcomed strangers but now entombs her memories. Old, mottled photographs line the walls and herald in the past, declaring the loss, the stolen opportunities, and the unfulfilled promises. As she examines the contents of the frames, she ponders on her life. One can only take so much disappointment. One can only take so many blows before it is time to leave the ring. She was right to store her dreams away in a box and hang up her hopes like garments in a musty, forgotten cupboard. She was right all along. Every experience she had only confirmed her insignificance, her unworthiness.

As her clouded eyes search the images, she is relieved she didn't put her hopes in unattainable pinnacles. Yes, she did do the right thing. Glancing over the photographs of times past, she knows that her life has been as dull as the sepia photos before her, her life a wasteland where her dreams lie decayed and long forgotten. 'It is the way it is supposed to be' are the words that invade her thoughts. Others are lucky enough to have a straight path to walk upon. They get the fulfilled hopes. She has ceased to envy those who achieved her dreams, who received her deepest desires. Yes, she was right to accept her fate before she was deceived into thinking that something better awaited her. Those who expect nothing, lose nothing. Those who guard their hearts experience less pain. Yes, she was right to board up her heart as she boarded up her home, her world.

In a gloom of self-pity, her heart oppressed, the woman turns from the captured moments of her colourless life and begins to climb the stairs to her bedroom. Her age calls to her as she takes the difficult journey, carefully and slowly climbing one step at a time as boards creak beneath her. It's a journey that's as difficult as her life's journey has been. She sets her foot on the rung of rejection and remembers her lost love. She was forsaken for another, her inner beauty not seen.

Her next step lands on the rung of unforgiveness and she remembers the words spoken to her over a lifetime, words that have cut to her heart and cemented to her, her worth. The actions committed by others resound in her memory like a dripping tap, wearing away her peace.

Slowly, she reaches the rung of fear. She ponders on the lost opportunities, how she sabotaged her dreams by listening to her doubts and limitations. Next, she sets a fragile foot on the rung of disappointment, remembering how one door after another closed on her dreams and left stains that coloured her expectations.

Shifting her weight, she reaches the rung of grief. The loss of loved ones resounds within her heart and hardens it like cement. As she nears the end of her journey, she sets her foot on the rung of despair. All hope has been lost. Her fate has been sealed, brought on by her need to be right, to be in control, to remain safe, and to elude surprise and potential risks. Yes, she was right.

Finally, the woman reaches her destination and lies down on the bed that she herself has made. She knows every layer, every crease, every mark, and every stain. Familiarity makes her comfortable. In the stillness and the darkness, a sigh. She rests one hand upon the other, hands that have not given affection, hands that have not aided others. In the silence, she hears birds twittering, the leaves rustling, and the distant humming of progress and change. Life goes on. Opportunities lie in wait for others who are luckier than she. As she lies there, waiting, life leaves her feeble and aged frame. Finally, she gets what she expected.

Eventually, those who come to document the end of her journey walk down the moss-covered path, through the evergreen overgrowth, past the thorny bushes that stand as sentinels, and then . . . they walk through the unlocked door.

Afterword

Dear reader,

Thank you so much for persisting in reading my story. It blesses me more than I can say in words. The purpose of this book is to bring encouragement and hope to all who read it. To me, the best and only way to do so is to give you the opportunity to have your own relationship with God. If you have never asked the God of the Heavens and the Earth, the God of my heart, into yours, then by saying and believing with all your heart the prayer below, you too can experience the wonder, the love, peace, and joy that I have come to know. John 14:6 says, 'Jesus answered, "I am the way and the truth and the life. No one comes to the Father except through me."' It is through Christ that we receive salvation and eternal life. Romans 10:9-13 says:

If you confess with your mouth the Lord Jesus and believe in your heart that God has raised Him from the dead, you will be saved. For with the heart one believes unto righteousness, and with the mouth confession is made unto salvation. For the Scripture says, *"Whoever believes on Him will not be put to shame."* For there is no distinction between Jew and Greek, for the same Lord over all is rich to all who call upon Him. For *"whoever calls on the name of the LORD shall be saved."* (NKJV)

If you are willing to throw your life into the arms of the one and only God, the Creator of the universe and the Saviour of all who believe in Him, this prayer is for you:

'Lord, I understand that all have sinned and fallen short of Your glory (Romans 3:23), and I acknowledge that I am a sinner. I come to You now with an open heart and ask for forgiveness, believing that Jesus Christ is Your Son, and that He died on the cross to forgive my sins, rising again, and He now sits at Your right hand (Romans 8:34). I ask, Lord, that You would come and live within my heart. Come and invade my life, that I would know the peace, love, and joy that comes from being in a right relationship with You, my Creator. I desire to do Your will in my life. Lead me into Your will and purposes for my life. I ask these things in the precious name of Jesus Christ. Amen.'

Dear reader, if you have said this prayer for the first time, or you have surrendered your life back to God again, welcome to the family, and BIG HUGS! I would be doing a happy dance and crying if I were with you. My trials have been worth it if through reading this book you have been brought into right relationship with God and received salvation, finding the love, joy and peace that only comes through surrendering your life to Christ.

Blessed be the God and Father of our Lord Jesus Christ, who according to His abundant mercy has begotten us again to a living hope through the resurrection of Jesus Christ from the dead, to an inheritance incorruptible and undefiled and that does not fade away, reserved in heaven for you, who are kept by the power of God through faith for salvation ready to be revealed in the last time. In this you greatly rejoice, though now for a little while, if need be, you have been grieved by various trials, that the genuineness of your faith, being much more precious than gold that perishes, though it is tested by fire, may be found to praise, honor, and glory at the revelation of Jesus Christ, whom having not seen you love. Though now you do not see Him, yet believing, you rejoice with joy inexpressible and full of glory, receiving the end of your faith—the salvation of your souls.
1 Peter 1:3-9 (NKJV)

Bibliography

Always, Always Something Sings, Emerson, RW, (1803-1882), Poem, Unknown source.

For Those Who Wait, Fireflight, 2010, Song Copyright: Flicker Records, Franklin, TN.

The Holy Bible (King James Version), Public Domain.

The Holy Bible (New International Version), 1978, International Bible Society, NY.

The Holy Bible (New King James Version), 1982, Thomas Nelson, Nashville, TN.

The Holy Bible (New Living Translation), 1996, Tyndale House Publishers Inc, Ill.

How to Pray for Healing, Ahn, C, 2004, Regal Books, CA. *The Message Bible,* Peterson, EH, 2002, Navpress, CO. *There are always flowers,* Henri Matisse. BrainyQuote.com,

Xplore Inc, 2012. http://www.brainyquote.com/quotes/quotes/h/henrimatis109310.html, accessed January 16, 2012.

What lies before us, Henry David Thoreau. BrainyQuote.com, Xplore Inc, 2012. http://www.brainyquote.com/quotes/quotes/h/henrydavid145971.html, accessed January 16, 2012.

About the author

Author, Julie Tyrie, now named Julie Modra, remarried in September, 2018, nine and a half years after Neil's passing. She waited—sometimes impatiently—for the right man to come along, marrying a prince worthy of every romance story ever written. Julie and her husband's divinely orchestrated meet-cute and the evidence of God's hand in their union is a testament to God's faithfulness to care for and provide for His children.

Her three beautiful girls are excelling in life and are still devoted to God. Emmy has travelled the world as a model, having her father's height, and is now a devoted wife and mum. Julie relishes her role as 'Meema' to her beautiful grandchildren. Maya has grown into a kind, generous, and creative young lady who continues to push through all obstacles. She is still cancer-free and benefits daily from God's grace and faithfulness as she works with young children in childcare. Her life is a miracle. Callie also has her dad's height but takes after her mother in her love of literature and the classics. She is a powerhouse, led by her drive for justice and championing the underdog. Julie and her family still reside in the beautiful bayside city of Redlands, Queensland.

In recent years, Julie retired from teaching and returned to study, learning the craft of fiction writing, as well as editing. She is now a full-time author, writing inspirational, Christian literary fiction with the purpose of encouraging readers with messages of hope, making widely known her Heavenly Daddy's unfailing love and faithfulness.

You can follow Julie's author journey and find information about her books on her website: juliemodra.com. You can also follow Julie on Facebook and Instagram. She would LOVE to hear from you.

Left: Me at approx. 6 years of age

Below: Maya's first birthday whilst in hospital

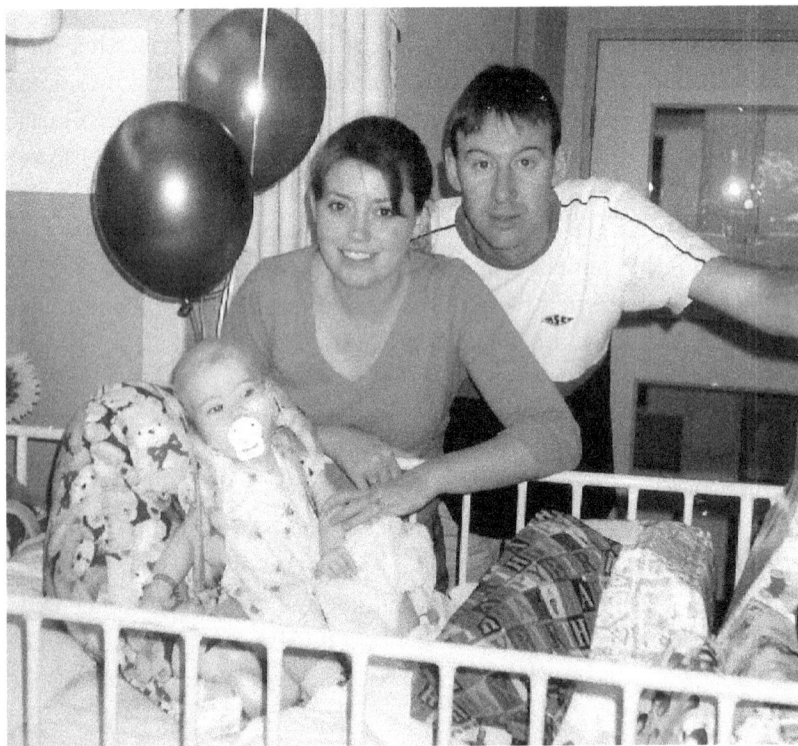

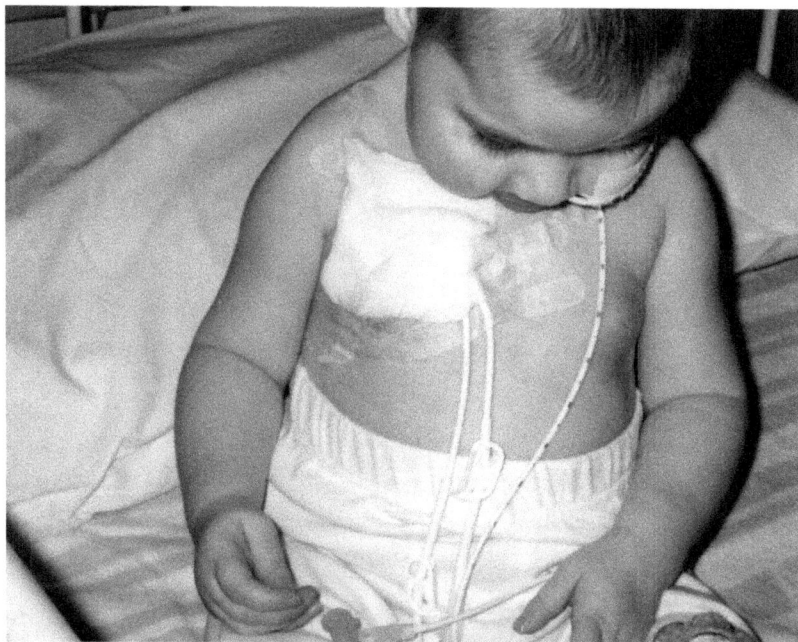

Above: Maya with her central line
Below: Neil and Emmy with Maya before she lost her hair

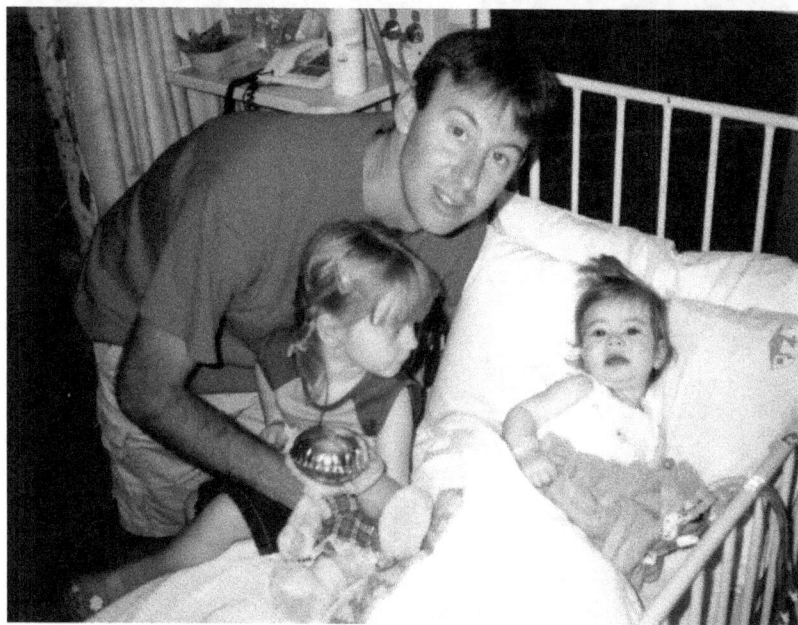

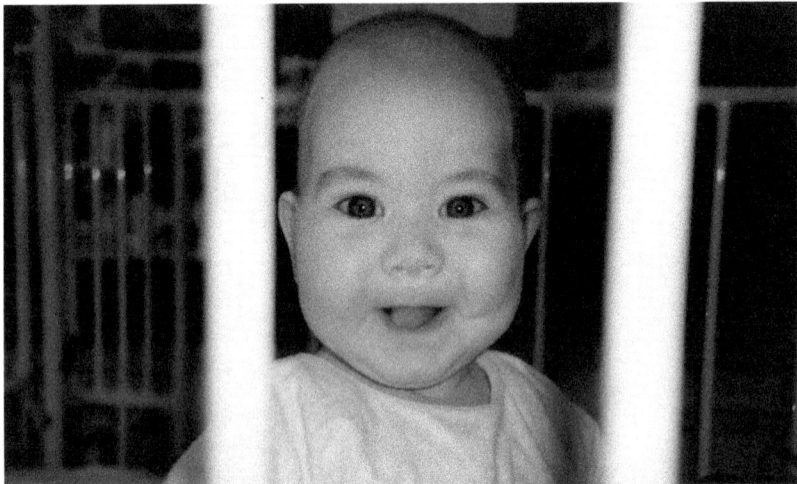

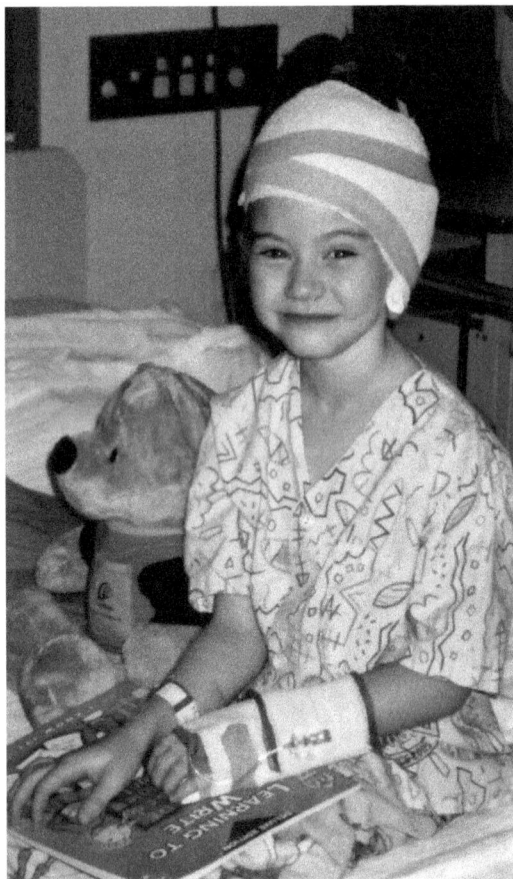

Above: Maya minus her hair with a puffy face from the fluids

Right: Maya's first cochlear ear implant in 2006, aged 6 years old

Above: A family outing in the hospital grounds at Westmead;
Below: Christmas 2007

Above: Neil, Emmy, Maya and Callie at the zoo... sick from chemotherapy that day;
Below: Maya and Callie walking with Dad at Bunyah Mountains

Above: Neil and the girls having a grass fight at Bunyah Mountains February 2008; Below: Neil pretending to be sick on his first day of chemotherapy

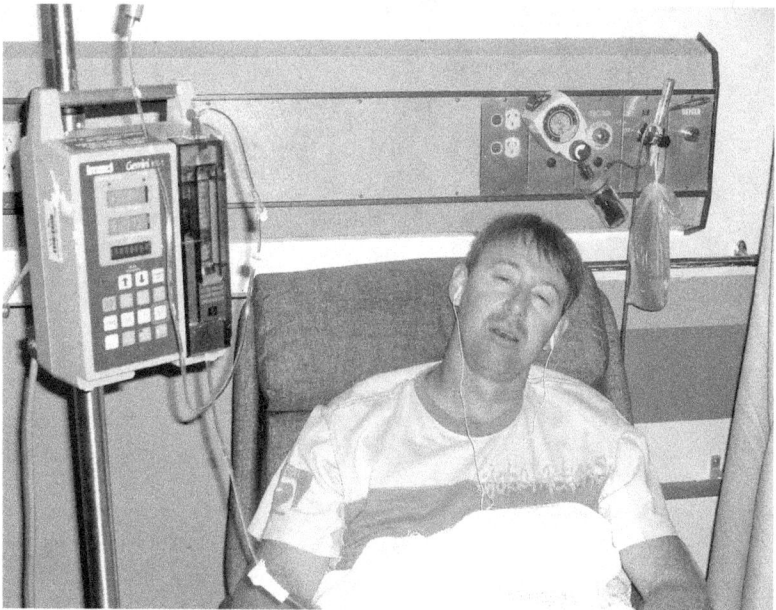

Above: Christmas Day 2008. Three days before Neil's stroke

Above: Neil in hospital with Maya, Emmy and Callie February 2009
Below: Neil home from the hospital in February 2009

www.ingramcontent.com/pod-product-compliance
Lightning Source LLC
LaVergne TN
LVHW051556080426
835510LV00020B/2997